For Lou.

Louie Läuger

Rethinking Gender
An Illustrated Exploration

The MIT Press
Cambridge, Massachusetts
London, England

Originally published as *Gender-Kram: Illustrationen und Stimmen zu Geschlecht*
© 2020, Unrast Verlag

The translation of this work was supported by a grant from the Goethe-Institut.

The MIT Press would like to thank the anonymous peer reviewers who provided comments on drafts of this book. The generous work of academic experts is essential for establishing the authority and quality of our publications. We acknowledge with gratitude the contributions of these otherwise uncredited readers.

This book was set in Josefin Sans, Trailmade, Shadows into Light and BadaBoom Pro BB by Louie Läuger.
Printed and bound in the United States of America.

Library of Congress Cataloging-in-Publication Data.

Names: Läuger, Louie, author.
Title: Rethinking gender : an illustrated exploration / Louie Läuger.
Other titles: Gender-Kram. English
Description: [Cambridge] : [The MIT Press], [2022] | "Originally published as Gender-Kram: Illustrationen und Stimmen zu Geschlecht © 2020, Unrast Verlag"–Title page verso.
Identifiers: LCCN 2021062385 (print) | LCCN 2021062386 (ebook) | ISBN 9780262047234 (paperback) | ISBN 9780262371179 (epub) | ISBN 9780262371186 (pdf)
Subjects: LCSH: Gender identity. | Gender nonconformity. | Gender expression.
Classification: LCC HQ18.55 .L3813 2022 (print) | LCC HQ18.55 (ebook) | DDC 305.3–dc23/eng/20220127
LC record available at https://lccn.loc.gov/2021062385
LC ebook record available at https://lccn.loc.gov/2021062386

10 9 8 7 6 5 4 3 2 1

Contents

1
The Basics

Gender is a ridiculously complicated topic.

Thinking about your own gender identity is hard enough. Understanding the gender of others? That seems impossible sometimes.

This book is here to help!

Things you should know about this book:

- There is more to learn than what's in this book!
- It's not free of mistakes.
- It will not explain the "wrong" or "right" ways to think of gender. (Because what is wrong or right, really?)

Sorry about that!

The question "What even is gender?" can be answered in more than one way. I want to show you some possible perspectives and answers in this book.

You can think of this book as a sort of map of the landscape of gender.

Or as a notebook that helps you reflect on your own gender.

Or as a toolbox that might help you empathize with others.

Or just simply as a good, old-fashioned book.

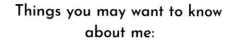

Things you may want to know about me:

That's me!
HI!
My name is Louie and I'm an illustrator and author based in Germany. I like coffee and feminism.

This is my cat. Her name is Cat and she really doesn't care about gender.

This is the point of view I'm writing from:

I have white privilege.

I was raised traditionally feminine.

This book was created as part of my master's degree.

I am an activist in intersectional feminist communities.

I am queer. (What that means is explained on the next page.)

English is my second language.

A CHEAT SHEET

A lot of the terms I'm using might be new for you. That's fine! Don't worry about it! When I started reading up on gender it was super intimidating to me: I didn't understand half of the things people talked about. It felt like having to learn vocabulary for a new language. That's why I will try to explain every complicated word when it first comes up in this book.

To make life a little easier for all of us I created this cheat sheet. Obviously, everything on there is condensed, shortened, and incomplete. At the end I left some space for your own notes and definitions. (Yes, you are allowed or even invited to write in this book.) You can also skip this page and come back to it in case you need it later.

The important, scary and big words.

AFAB/AMAB - Acronyms for "assigned/assumed female at birth" / "assigned/assumed male at birth." Describes the gender a person was assigned at birth.

Cis, cisgender - The gender of a cis person aligns with the one they were assigned at birth.

Dysphoria - This term is used to describe the discomfort or pain people experience when their gender does not align with the one they were assigned at birth.

Endo - A person who is not -> inter. Alternative terms for endo(sex) are peri(sex) and dyadic. The language to descirbe non-inter people is still evolving and changing.

Gender - When interpreted as binary, the social construct of male and female. All the social and cultural expectations being put on a person because of the gender assigned to them.

- The identity a person has. Examples are male, female, non-binary, agender, maverique, or graygender.

Inter - The sex characteristics of an inter or intersex person don't neatly fit into the medical categories of "male" or "female" bodies. More about that starting on page 25.

Intersectionality - A concept that helps us understand the specific experiences of people being discriminated against on multiple axes. For example, how someone's experience changes if their reality is shaped by both racism and sexism.

LGBTQIA+ - Stands for lesbian, gay, bisexual, trans, queer, inter, agender/asexual. The + symbolizes other sexual orientations and gender identities within the community.

Sex - Whereas gender describes the social construct, sex refers to biology. The biological characteristics we consider to be male or female. This whole concept is debatable; you can find more out about all that in the second chapter.

Trans - The gender of a trans person does not align with the gender they were assigned at birth. Sometimes also described as transsexual or transgender.

Transition - Describing a phase of change. May be a social, legal, and/or medical transition regarding one's gender perception or expression.

Queer - The word has no fixed definition. Formerly a slur, it has been reclaimed by the community. It's an umbrealla term often used synonymously with the acronym "LGBTQIA+."

What we know about gender and sex, as a society, is still growing and evolving. Every person has a slightly different understanding of gender — yours is probably different from mine. And instead of arguing about who's right, I'd like to ask: What can we learn from each other?

I often have to remind myself to remain patient. It's okay that I don't know everything. It's okay to be learning and to make mistakes on the way.

Where to find me:

@tenderrebellions

tenderrebellions.com

Quite a few people looked through this book to make it as inclusive as we possibly could. Huge thanks to Anna, Sabrina, and Tascha from *innenAnsicht magazine, Noah and Nick from RosaLinde Leipzig, and my editor Matt.

Nonetheless some mistakes will probably remain in this book. If you can't see yourself anywhere on these pages: Tell me about it! After publishing this book, I will continue creating work around gender and uplifting the voices of marginalized people. (Marginalized people are those pushed to the margins of society.) A lot of it you can find online and through Instagram.

SEX & GENDER

There are so many concepts around sex and gender, it's sometimes hard to keep track of what we're talking about. We'll get into some of these concepts in depth in a bit — for now let's map out some of the stuff connected with these words:

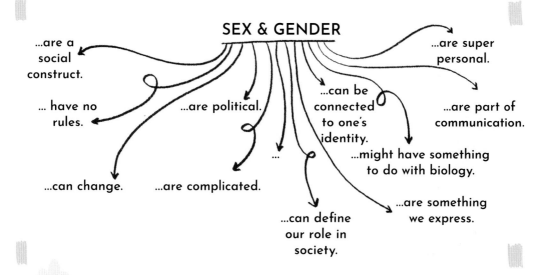

SEX & GENDER

...are a social construct.

... have no rules.

...are political.

...can be connected to one's identity.

...

...can change.

...are complicated.

...can define our role in society.

...might have something to do with biology.

...are something we express.

...are super personal.

...are part of communication.

The whole thing can be confusing and emotional. In this book we'll go through it bit by bit.

If you feel overwhelmed at any point: Feel free to skip sections. Take some breaks. Or read this book with your friends.

Especially when we're thinking about such a personal and significant thing as gender, it's important to be kind and loving with ourselves. So take all the time you need!

This is how people imagined gender for a long time. Our parents and maybe even we ourselves grew up with these two options.

Today a lot of people see gender as a spectrum. Maybe you remember images of electromagnetic spectrums from school.

The spectrum of daylight looks something like this.

Gender and sex don't have to be all-or-nothing choices.

Imagining gender as a spectrum has the advantage that it changes our perception a little bit. Everything becomes more flexible; nothing has to be 100% and new possibilities become visible.

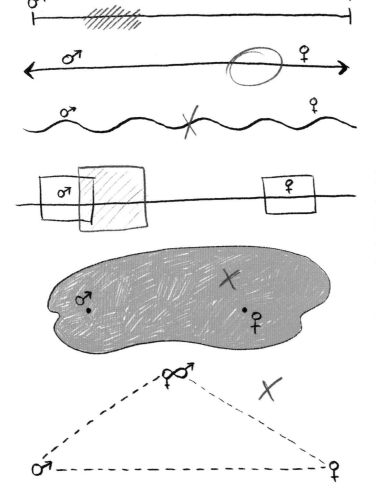

A spectrum and where you are on that spectrum can be drawn in a lot of different ways. None of these depictions is perfect. They are just models, here to help us grasp something that our brains find complicated. If these drawings are helpful to you, feel free to sketch them next to the following explanatory texts. If they are more confusing to you, just ignore them. Take what you need and leave the rest.

Different people experience gender very differently. One thing that plays a huge role in that is a concept called "intersectionality."

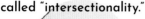
Ain't I a woman?

The activist Sojourner Truth gave a famous speech with the title "Ain't I a Woman?" in 1851. The sentence was later picked up by the author bell hooks.

Both wanted to bring attention to their unique and too often ignored experience as Black women. Anti-racist movements mostly centered the needs of Black men while feminist communities were heavily focused on the problems of white women.

Inter-sectionality describes how discrimination overlaps for some people. If a person is affected by several different forms of marginalization, their experience is shaped in very specific ways. For example: The experience of a Black lesbian woman is different from the experience of a white woman using a wheelchair. Sexism affects them differently, even though both of them are women.

The feminist and professor Kimberlé Crenshaw coined the term "intersectionality."

An intersectional approach helps us better understand complex topics and be more inclusive when we talk about social justice.

I like to imagine intersectionality as a ball of tangled threads. If you just start pulling wherever you will make a mess. Instead, you have to figure out how the threads intersect.

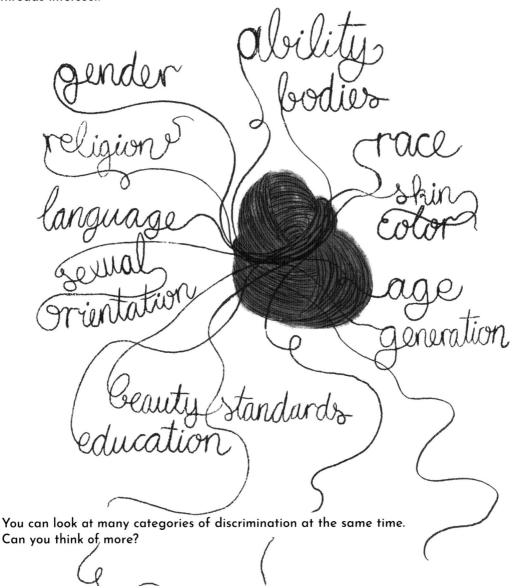

You can look at many categories of discrimination at the same time. Can you think of more?

Talking about discrimination gets incredibly complicated when you first include an intersectional approach. (Don't worry, you'll get the hang of it!)

A woman using a wheelchair might only be seen for her disability, and not as a person with a gender and sexual orientation.

A woman wearing a hijab might be perceived as someone who is oppressed by her husband and can't be her own person.

In reality I am idependent and exercise agency. My free choices are invisible to you, thanks to your prejudice.

I can have romantic and sexual relationships if I want to.

A fat woman might be labeled as unhygienic, lazy, or ugly.

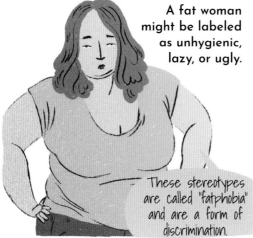

These stereotypes are called "fatphobia" and are a form of discrimination.

These women experience discrimination very differently from one another, because their gender intersects with other factors. That also means that it is possible for one person to be discriminated against because of some parts of their identity but be privileged because of others.

It is important to remind ourselves: Our experiences are not the same as everyone else's. We can't draw conclusions based solely on our own lives.

2
Sex Assigned at Birth

The first aspect of gender we're going to explore is biology. I'm starting here not because it's the most important thing, but because a lot of people find it easiest to grasp: We are looking at bodies.

We often talk about "sex" rather than "gender" when we talk about biology. Another term is "sex assigned at birth." We say "assigned" because when you were born a doctor decided: It's a girl./It's a boy.

Congratulations, It's a...

This assignment is based on the newborn's genitalia.

If the child has a vulva, it's assigned "girl."

If the child has a penis, it's assigned "boy."

I am saying that, when sex is assigned at birth, what actually happens is: we're assigning gender. Gender is explored in the next chapter, where we'll talk more about how and why that assignment might be off. But just to be clear: no matter how often we say "assigned sex," we're still assigning gender based on visible bodily traits and calling that sex.

Your sex actually has a lot more biological characteristics than just genitalia.

20

	A	B	C
I have...	...a vulva.	...a penis.	...both/neither/ I don't know.
I menstruate/used to menstruate/would menstruate if I wasn't on the pill.	Yes.	No.	I don't know (yet).
I have testicles.	No.	Yes.	Maybe?
I have a uterus.	Yes.	No.	No idea.
My body produces...	...more estrogen than testosterone.	...more testosterone than estrogen.	I really don't know.
My chromosomes are...	XX	XY	Should I know this?
When I went through puberty, my voice "broke."	Not noticeably.	Yes./Surely soon!	I don't know (yet).
I can grow a beard.	No.	Yes./A little bit.	Not yet./I don't know.
I have visible boobs.	Yes.	No.	Not yet./I'm not sure.
My shoulders are...	...small.	...wide.	Neither./I can't tell.

First question: A	First question: B	Mostly C
You were probably assigned female at birth.	You were probably assigned male at birth.	It's okay to be unsure and not know yet. We're going to explore throughout this book what it could mean if you have a lot of mixed answers.

In our society, humans get sorted into two categories ("men" and "women") based on their genitalia. We made these categories up. Sure, bodies are different from each other; I'm not arguing against that. I'm just saying: Sorting bodies in two boxes and labeling one woman and the other one man — that was our idea. We could have come up with a completely different system! For example:

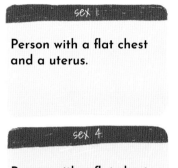

sex 1

Person with a flat chest and a uterus.

sex 2

Person with boobs and a uterus.

sex 3

Person with a uterus and testicles.

sex 4

Person with a flat chest and testicles.

sex 5

Person with boobs and testicles.

sex 6

Person with other characteristics.

That's why I like the term "sex assigned at birth". It makes it visible that this whole assignment is an active process. You weren't just assigned a sex (or gender) by accident.

Being assigned a sex doesn't mean you have to identify with it for the rest of your life (or ever). Also, the assignment might have been wrong. We'll talk about intersex and trans people in a bit!

Remember the idea of gender as a spectrum? (If you don't, you can look at page 14 again.) Sex characteristics are also a spectrum!

Here are just a few examples. The size and shape of genitalia are different for each person. The same goes for where body fat sits or the amount of hormones your body produces.

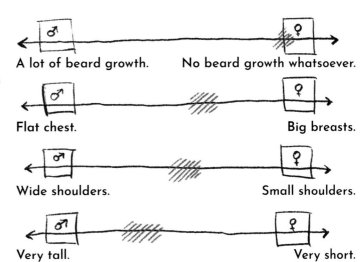

A lot of beard growth.   No beard growth whatsoever.

Flat chest.   Big breasts.

Wide shoulders.   Small shoulders.

Very tall.   Very short.

Most bodies don't fit neatly into one of the two boxes for every category we can look at.

Bodies are very different from each other – even those assigned the same sex at birth.

AFAB people who can grow a beard exist. So do AMAB people with breasts.

Biology is a lot more ambiguous than it seems at first glance.

How important biology is to you is something you'll have to decide for yourself.

PCOS, for example, is a metabolic disorder. One of the symptoms is hair growth on the face. This doesn't mean I am less of a woman.

Östrogen

$C_{18}H_{24}O_2$

Testosteron

$C_{19}H_{28}O_2$

MIX & MATCH

Not every person fits into our medicalized categories of "male" and "female." If you can think of a combination of sex characteristics, it probably exists.

INTERSEX

Congratulations! It's a... I don't know exactly?

Intersex or just "inter" people were born with bodies that don't fit in our two-boxes system. An inter person might have a vulva but internal testicles. Or a penis and XX chromosomes. Or a vagina and breasts but more testosterone than estrogen.

Here is a question we maybe shouldn't be asking but a lot of people are still interested in:

Is this really important? Surely this doesn't affect a lot of people!

"Intersex" is a term for all the variations from our traditional understanding of sex. That doesn't mean these variations have to fall exactly in the middle between "male" and "female."

Currently it is estimated that 1 in 200 people is intersex. Speaking of percentages: This is as many people with naturally red hair! But it doesn't really matter how many people are affected. It is important to take their needs seriously and protect their rights – even or especially if it's only a small group.

With most intersex people you won't know that they are inter if they don't tell you. A lot of intersex people fit into our ideas of male and female when we just look at them. And how often do you ask people about their genitalia or chromosomes?

I have inner testicles. But you can't see that from the outside and I don't have to tell you if I don't want to.

Sometimes it's clear at birth that the child is intersex. Sometimes a person finds out later in life, for example if they don't start to menstruate when they expected to. Or even later than that, for example when they can't have a child and try to find out why.

Some terms inter people might be using:

IAFAB - Intersex aassigned female at birth.

IAMAB - Intersex assigned male at birth.

FAFAB - Forcibly assigned female at birth.

FAMAB - Forcibly assigned male at birth.

Intersex people don't have to use or identify with these words. Some use them to describe their specific experiences. Whether or not an inter person uses these words is completely up to them.

In case you were wondering: "Wait, why are you saying forcibly assigned??" here's a little history lesson.

In France the media brought a lot of attention to an intersex person. Herculine Barbin was forced to live as a man and called a "monster" in the newspaper. They took their own life when they were 29.

1860s

1917

Richard Goldsmith used the term "intersex" the way we use it today for the first time. Before that, the word was used to describe the relationship between the sexes. Inter people were called "hermaphrodites" until that point.

A lot of people think "hermaphrodite" is derogatory today, so only use it to describe someone if they use that word to describe their identity. And even then, you should check in with them first whether it's okay for you to use the word as well. Especially if yourself are endosex (that is, not intersex).

1950S

Intersex people are healthy. But I'm sure they would do even better if they fit into our ideas of gender and sex.

I am a psychologist and know what I'm talking about! You can trust me, I wrote hundreds of articles about intersex people!

Dr. John Money was convinced that gender is only a question of upbringing. His theory: The sex of newborns can be decided up until they are eighteen months old. His "proof": After an accident during a circumcision, a baby was operated on and was afterward raised as a girl, no problem.

Thirty years later that baby started living as a man. Dr. Money didn't really care, though.

Before the 1950s, intersex adults could more or less decide themselves whether or not they wanted to have any sort of surgery. Dr. John Money fundamentally changed how intersex people are treated in our medical system. He started the still ongoing trend of so-called normalizing surgeries for intersex babies and children.

Why am I doing this? Well, it's obvious: How can an intersex person have a clear sexual orientation? Only someone who is clearly male or female can avoid becoming homosexual. Because I don't only dislike inter people, I also have something against gays.

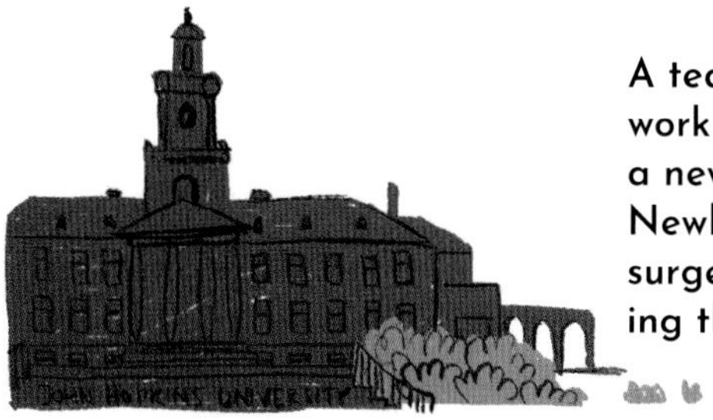

A team at Johns Hopkins University continued the work started by Dr. John Money and implemented a new standard in the treatment of inter people. Newborns and babies now received "normalizing" surgeries on a regular basis – often without notifying the parents.

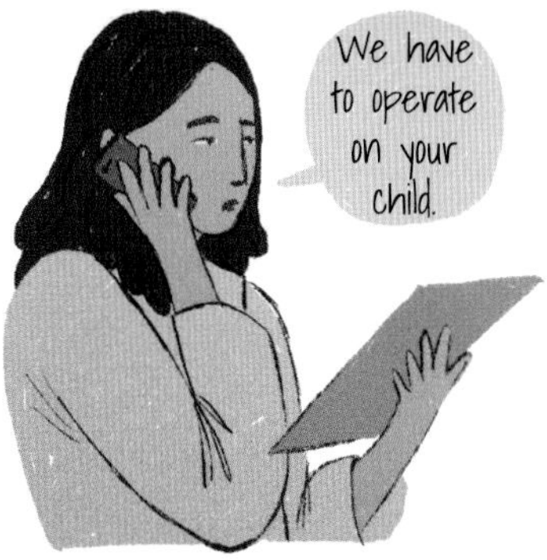
We have to operate on your child.

Doctors typically said there was an issue with hearing or other internal organs, to get consent from the parents for surgery.

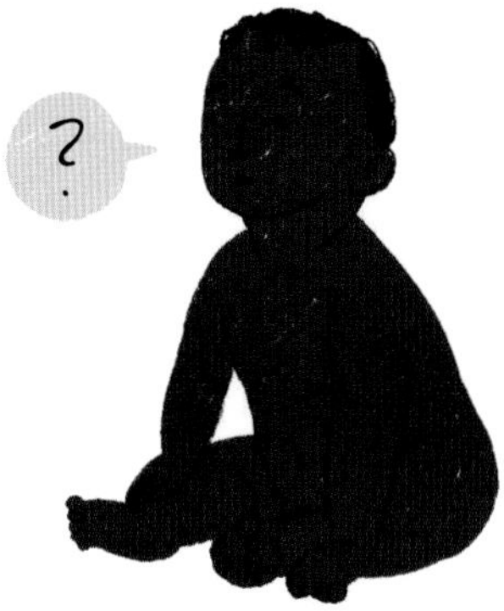
?

The real reason wasn't disclosed to the parents. And, of course, the children also weren't told.

Parents who did know about their child being intersex mostly got this piece of advice:

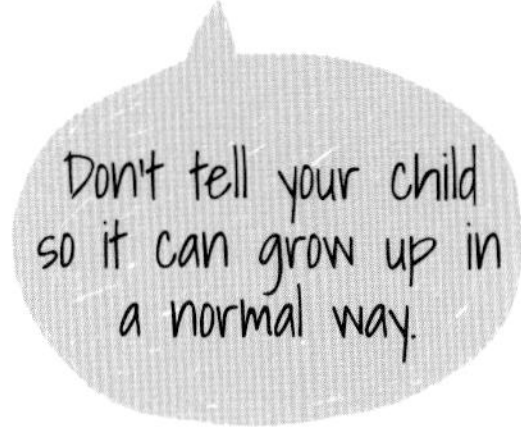
Don't tell your child so it can grow up in a normal way.

Many intersex people found out only later in life about their medical history. The stigmatization of the topic made it so taboo that intersex people themselves were – and, in many cases, still are – struggling to come to terms with their being intersex.

1980S

Intersex people started building a community.

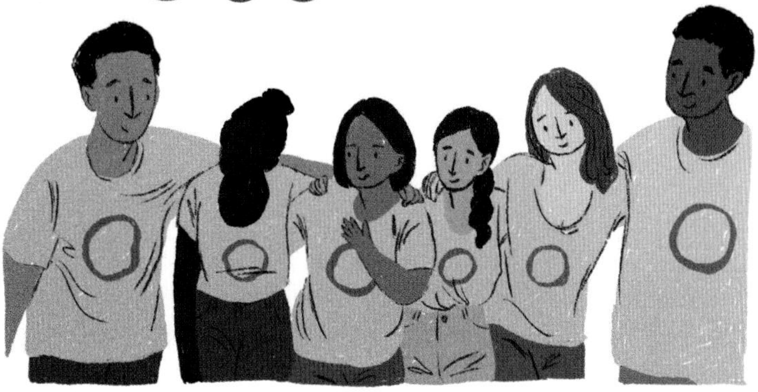

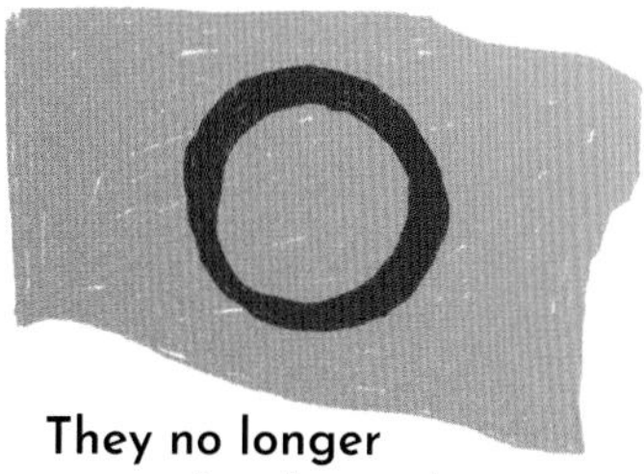

They no longer wanted to keep their identities a secret. The inter community became a place without shame or guilt. Their symbol is a yellow flag with a violet circle.

1993

In 1993, activist Cheryl Chase wrote an open letter announcing the founding of the Intersex Society of North America (ISNA). The open letter was later published by several magazines.

> I wrote a letter to the editor talking about my experience. The letter came out in "The Sciences" and announced the formation of the Intersex Society. Right away the mailbox started to fill up with letters from people whose stories are very much like mine. Not in the exact details, but in terms of being treated as shameful, lied to and being subjected to surgeries which they, as adults, deeply regret happening.[1]

In 1996, the first demonstration for the rights of intersex people took place!

The ISNA protested because of a medical congress in Boston. October 26 later became "Intersex Awareness Day": a yearly date to pay extra attention to issues important to the intersex community.

OCTOBER 26, 1996

The protesters wanted to reclaim the word "hermaphrodite." So they printed the phrase "Hermaphrodites with attitude" on T-shirts, posters, and flyers.

When the activists started working with medical professionals to stop the surgeries, the word "intersex" was established as the go-to term.

[1]Cheryl Chase quoted in in Peter Hegarty, "Intersex Activism, Feminism and Psychology: Opening a Dialogue on Theory, Research and Clinical Practice," *Feminism & Psychology* 10, no. 1 (2000):117–132.

To this day intersex people fight for more education and awareness around their existence and to stop invasive medical treatments.

2006

DR. HOUSE

The TV show *House* picked up the topic of being intersex in one of its episodes. A girl was the center of the story. The fictional doctor found inner testicles and diagnosed: "Oh, it's really a boy." The show was criticized after airing this episode. It reinforced the idea that there are a couple of categories that determine your sex. For a lot of intersex people, it's really important not to be forced into one of those two categories.

For the show *Faking It* the organization Interact worked with MTV. Together they created the character of Lauren Cooper, an intersex girl who is trying to navigate femininity and sexuality while struggling with her identity as intersex person.

I was born with XY chromosomes but developed as a girl, okay? The pills I'm taking, it's estrogen, because my body doesn't produce any. There. Now you know.

2014

A THIRD OPTION

On questionnaires I often fail at the second question. I have to decide: man or woman. And once again, I don't feel seen, somehow ignored.

No medical expert, psychologist, or law can tell me I don't exist as a hermaphrodite. Whenever I look in the mirror, I see proof to the contrary.

After meeting more people who feel this way, some amazing supporters and I decided to do something.

This is Vanja from the German campaign "Third Option." Their campaign fights for the visibility and rights of intersex people.

The activists clearly state: There aren't two "natural" sexes or genders. The gender binary only exists because every person not fitting in is labeled as ill or unhealthy. This process is also called "pathologization."

The surgeries on intersex children need to end. Even the UN said they are a violation of human rights. And yet these surgeries continue to be performed in many parts of the world.

To protect and strengthen the rights of inter and trans people, Vanja started the Third Option campaign in 2013. In 2016, Vanja went to court and filed a constitutional complaint. The judge ruled in their favor! Not having a third option and legally recognizing intersex people violates equal rights for all sexes. As a result, politicians had to come up with a new law. Since 2018 the legal gender markers in Germany are "male," "female," and "diverse."

Another activist fighting for the rights of inter people is Lucie Veith. In 2004 Lucie Veith founded an association of intersex people. The association was based on a self-help group: women with XY chromosomes realized that all of them had traumatic experiences with medical treatments. A majority of intersex people undergo unnecessary surgeries. That's why the association focuses on the physical integrity of intersex people. Back in 2008 Lucie Veith and their organization put together the first nationwide report on the treatment of intersex people in Germany to educate others and raise awareness.

Intersex people worldwide are still confronted with discrimination and dehumanizing medical treatments. Activists are fighting to make sure this changes.

Our demands as an association of intersex people:
1. No medical treatments that aren't necessary to preserve health or life without informed consent.
2. Implementing new standards of care – in collaboration with intersex people.
3. Making sure intersex people are included in education.
4. Compensation for intersex people affected by these surgeries.
5. Integrating intersex into existing legislation.

Today many countries have laws meant to protect intersex people. In Germany doctors need consent from the parents to operate on newborns. Nonetheless these surgeries still take place. A study by Ruhr-University Bochum found out that in Germany about 1,800 of these surgeries are performed per year. On average that is five "normalizing," invasive procedures every day.

This treatment is the best thing you can do for your child.

As parents we trust in the opinion of medical professionals and therefore consent.

A lot of doctors who recommend the surgery don't do so because they hate intersex people or have bad intentions. They themselves simply aren't thoroughly educated on the matter. They are convinced they are acting in the best interests of the child.

These doctors often are convinced that the positive results of a "normalizing" surgery outweigh the negative ones. A lot of the time that is not the reality. And medically speaking most of these surgeries are not necessary for the health of the child. Therefore, intersex people demand that we hold off on such surgery until the child is old enough to decide for themselves.

Some doctors convince parents to agree to a surgery by telling them that being intersex results in an increased risk for cancer.

The possible side effects of the surgery are discussed much less by comparison.

For example, the body may not be able to regulate its hormones anymore, which can result in serious health problems. Many intersex people have to take hormones for the rest of their lives.

The surgery might assign the child a gender they later don't identify with.

Some surgeries result in a lack of libido.

The treatment may have negative effects on the mental health of the child. Many intersex people describe the experience as traumatic.

Surgeries and hormone treatments allow parents and doctors to believe the child is no longer intersex. With that argument they justify keeping the medical history a secret from the intersex person.

Many intersex people feel isolated, ashamed, alone, or guilty. So it is even more important that endosex (non-intersex) people recognize these truths:

- Being intersex is not a new phenomenon that people just invented.
- Intersex bodies are not "less normal" or "weird" or "worth less."
- The intersex community exists. Intersex voices deserve to be heard and their needs are important and valid.

Dear intersex reader: You are amazing. Your body is magical. Nothing is wrong with you or your body and you don't have to become more "normal." Every change you make should be your free choice. You are a wonderful and lovable human being as you are and decide to be.

ON THE LEVEL OF BIOLOGY WE ARE ACTUALLY MORE SIMILAR THAN WE ARE DIFFERENT.

It is easy to forget this. Yes, our bodies are different in many ways. But in the end it's the same hormones making us emotional. It's the same organs keeping us alive. It's the same nervous systems allowing us to navigate this world.

We are still learning new things about biology. Not too long ago the idea of sex differences in the brain was discredited.

So how about we start talking about the things we have in common instead of creating a huge divide based on small differences?

Space for your own notes:
How do you feel about biological characteristics that are frequently thought of as determining your sex? What do you think about getting rid of boxes and replacing them with spectrums? Did you learn about intersex people in school?

3
Gender as a Social Construct

GENDER IS A SOCIAL CONSTRUCT!

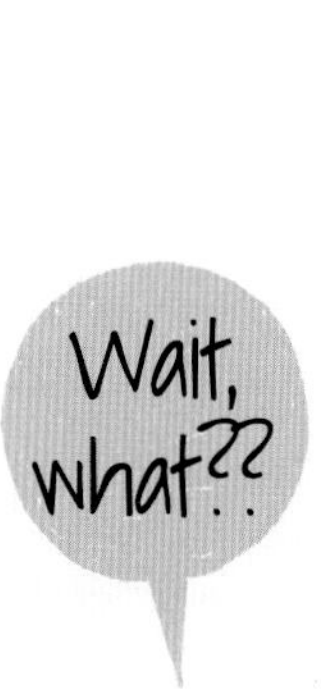

This claim gets thrown around a lot, especially in feminist communities. Let's figure out what it means!

Sex is our system of categorizing bodies into "male" and "female" based on medicalized norms. Gender is about social and cultural aspects of our identity and our role in society. We expect different things based on the assignment that took place at birth. And all these gender roles often start right at birth, or even before.

And even though neither sex nor gender are binary we only construct two, binary options. Everything and everyone are either "male" or "female" in our social and cultural construct of gender.

Congratulations!
It's a...

...human?

Gender as a social construct means we sort kids into blue and pink boxes full of pirates and princesses.

Gender means we expect girls and boys to behave in different ways.

Can you think of more characteristics than the ones I've listed below? What did you learn about boy- and girl-behavior? Add your own adjectives if you want to.

Girls are...

- emotional
- passive
- hysterical
- empathetic
- good listeners
- pretty
-
-
-

Boys are...

- logical thinkers
- rational
- active
- wild
- loud
- chaotic
-
-
-

Children understand rather quickly what gender we have assigned to them and what expectations come with it. Some time between kindergarten and primary school kids begin to understand gender roles. They know what type of behavior is expected from them and what they shouldn't be doing.

There are social ideas and norms around gender.

Kids learn these norms.

Children want to please the adults in their life by behaving in line with the norms.

Skills are developed accordingly.

Interests and hobbies fit into gender roles.

The child creates their own identity around ideas of "I am good at this thing; that other one, not so much."

And there you go, these small humans grow up into people with a very clear idea of femininity and masculinity and continue sharing these norms with the next generation.

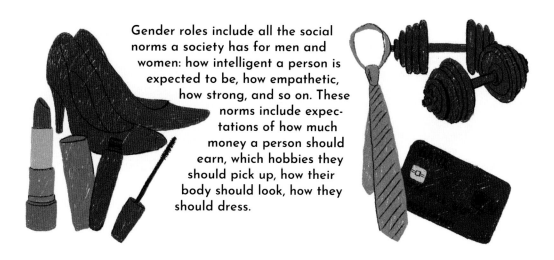

Gender roles include all the social norms a society has for men and women: how intelligent a person is expected to be, how empathetic, how strong, and so on. These norms include expectations of how much money a person should earn, which hobbies they should pick up, how their body should look, how they should dress.

Some societies, speficially Western European and North American countries, have developed ideals about men and women that look a little like this:

short hair

sporty, muscular, strong

Is dominant and a good leader. Provides for his family.

I want to and can have sex with beautiful women all the time.

Whenever I'm not thinking about sex I'm thinking about sports.

If I ever want to get married I will be the one to buy the ring and propose.

I am romantically interested in men.

I want to have kids and I am able to give birth to them.

until I start raising a family I concern myself mainly with shopping and my looks.

long hair

makeup

Emotional, talks about feelings a lot.

super smooth legs

These ideals create roles in our society that are gendered. As a girl/boy/man/woman you have a limited choice. The options available to you also depend on the context you live in. I'll explain this in a bit.

The fashionista

The athlete

The businessman

The caretaker

The politician

The mother

The housewife

The logician

The entertainer

The roles you take on change over the course of your life. Your age, class, race, where you live, your social bubble – all of these factors influence the options you have.

Often we have a lot of roles at the same time. For example, I am a student, an artist, a feminist, a friend, an activist, ...

Looking at culture and history, we will notice that the roles within a society change a lot. Today we associate femininity with roles connected to emotions, care work, or beauty. In other places or times this was or still is different. (Examples come up on pages 49 and 60.)

The idea that men and women exist in opposition to each other and therefore have different roles and characteristics is called the gender binary. When we talk about the social contruct of this binary we often just call it gender or gender role.

This binary can be found in every aspect of our everyday life. Can you think of more than these few examples?

Women drink sparkling wine with strawberries; men want beer and steak.

Beauty products smell and look different for men and women.

Girls play with dolls; boys play with cars.

A lot of people believe that this binary is the natural state of the world and has something to do with DNA or our brains. Others are convinced it's only a question of upbringing. The truth is probably a bit more complicated.

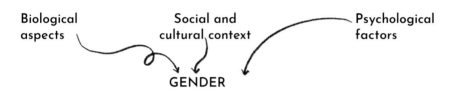

Biological aspects

Social and cultural context

Psychological factors

GENDER

How we treat people has consequences. Women today tend to be smaller than men because they did less physical labor in the past. It wasn't always like that. Some Viking skeletons suggest that people we would assign male and female at birth were around the same height and shoulder width back then.

Another example: Kids who are encouraged to play with toy building blocks develop different brain areas than the children encouraged to play with dolls.

Our social and cultural norms or expectations have a very real effect on our biology. So is gender really "natural" in any way?

The diagram above should perhaps look more like this:

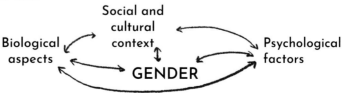

Social and cultural context

Biological aspects

Psychological factors

GENDER

The short answer:

SEXIST AND HETERO-NORMATIVE IDEAS ARE DIRECTLY TIED TO OUR CAPITALIST WAY OF LIFE.

To put it more simply:
Our ideas of gender give more power and opportunities to men. We also live in a world that assumes everyone is straight (heteronormativity). These ideals are connected to our profit-oriented economy.

Let's look at this answer in more depth.
When society was industrialized and we entered the so-called Age of Reason, a new physical separation resulted between work and home. Paid work was now done in factories.

The work going into enabling humans to perform paid labor was done at home. That work is also called care work. Examples include raising children, doing the laundry, cooking, taking care of elderly family members, getting groceries, cleaning ...

During the Industrial Revolution a lot of working class families couldn't afford this gendered separation. After the First World War there was an increased desire for a peaceful family life, which enforced this separation of labor.

While white men took over public spaces of paid work and politics, white women stayed at home. The justification given for this: women give birth, so it's only natural for them to stay at home and take care of the children.

Given the huge wage gaps between the white and BIPOC (Black, Indigenous, and People of Color) communities, this separation of labor held predominantly for white folks, as they were able to afford it. Black women weren't able to spend as much time on care work as society expected them to and white supremacy turned it into a racist stereotype about motherhood.

To this day women do significantly more of the care work than men. Often they do this on top of their paid work.

All of this care work can't be managed and organized in the same way as paid work. How should raising a child be more time efficient and profitable? Even if someone is hired to help out in the household, it is often a woman — often a women of color and/or an immigrant. And that hired woman is still doing the care work in her own home on top of the job.

Our economy would fall apart if the people who perform the vast majority of traditonally feminized care work collectively refused to continue doing so unpaid. One example of this is the women's strike in Iceland on October 24, 1975. Nearly all women in the country refused to work that day. And society pretty much came to a crashing halt.

To keep our economy going the way we do now, we have to believe that...

...women are better suited for care work than men.
...gender roles are "natural" and real and explained by biology.
...men provide for their family financially.
...only two genders exist.

(None of this is true.)

The gender binary keeps a power imbalance alive.

Of course other things play into power imbalances as well. But can we please stop with this binary way of thinking already?

By the way:
Before the "Age of Reason" people were convinced that only one gender exists and that women are merely "underdeveloped men." If we were able to change our perception of gender this radically before - why not do it again?

Why do humans even care so much about gender? Shouldn't everyone just live however they want to?

Place for your own notes:
What do you think about this separation of paid work and care work? Why do you think a lot of men don't participate in care work even today? Who does the care work in your own family? Which parts of care work are you doing yourself? How do you feel about it?

"You're only talking about isolated incidents, stop exaggerating this into a whole thing."

Sadly a lot of people are affected in very real ways by discrimination. Yes, sexism, racism, and classism show up in very personal ways in our everyday life. But they are also deeply rooted in our society and institutions.

"Girls are just not good with math."

A 2019 study found out that boys and girls are equally good in math. What remained the same: everyone expecting girls to do poorly. Which of course affects their confidence and performance.

"It' always been this way! Even back in the Stone Age!"

It's actually not true that humans in the stone age separated hunting and gathering by gender.

GENDER MYTHS

"All these new gender identities ... isn't that just a bunch of woke kids on the internet who want attention?"

Different ideas around gender have always existed, both in gender roles as well as gender identities. Kids on the internet are creative, but they aren't the first generation to think beyond gender binary.

"The female brain works differently. That doesn't have anything to do with any social construct."

The way our brain works has a lot to do with social context. We develop the skills that are demanded and encouraged. Whether you are interested in baseball or ballet (or both!), makeup or computer games (or both!), has very little to do with DNA.

Okay, let's say you now agree that this gender binary is actually crappy and no person should behave according to assigned gender roles. Well, I've got complicated news for you:

We all grew up in this binary.

Childhood experiences and toys

Binary restrooms

Gender marketing (products being marketed to a specific gender)

Role models

Media representation

Can you think of more?

We internalized all of these ideas about how women and men are supposed to be. So we probably have a lot of unconscious stereotypes that we actively need to unlearn.

The way we think is influenced by the gender binary, whether we want it to be or not. Simply coming to the conclusion that the binary doesn't have to be reality is not enough to free us from it. So we have so start an ongoing process of questioning, talking, and reflecting.

As a woman I should shave my legs before leaving the house.

...wait.

That's nonsense!

As a man I can't cry when watching romantic comedies.

Stop.

Of course I can!

(colleagues, family, friends, strangers)

Our experience of gender isn't something isolated from the rest of the world. Gender roles affect the image we have of ourselves, as well as the images others have of us and how they treat us.

How do different contexts affect your gender experience? How do you express your gender with different people? Which gendered expectations do you have in different scenarios for others?

When thinking about family, I expect more care work from my mother, and would be more likely to ask my father for career advice. Around friends I am queerer than at university. In classes I want to be one of the strong and confident female-assumed people.

This can look totally different for you. And it's only a glimpse of what you could note down here.

Family

Romantic and/or sexual relationships

Friendships

School/uni/work

Hobbies

Other

All these experiences around gender have very little to do with biology. Our experiences and expectations are based on the social construct of gender and cultural norms. (In this book I am talking about the ideas of gender we have in Western Europe and North America.)

Kids and teenagers are especially under a lot of pressure to live up to our gendered expectations.

The gender binary limits choices for all of us.

Children assigned female at birth who like soccer/math/technology are more likely to be labeled "unattractive" or "not very girly."

Children assigned male at birth who are interested in fashion or makeup, who like to dance and express themselves creatively, or who cry often get called a "pussy" or homophobic slurs.

How quickly we gender children's behavior was examined in the "Baby X" study. During the study people had to take care of two babies, one was dressed in blue, the other in pink.

When the baby in blue started screaming, participants said it's probably because of anger. When playing with these babies the participants didn't mention any worries or fear of accidentally hurting or overwhelming them.

Participants were also more likely to give dolls or stuffed animals to the babies dressed in pink. Their screams were answered with the question: "What's the matter?"

SiLENCE = DEATH

By the way, pink used to be a color symbolizing decisiveness and blue was considered to be more feminine and softer. This perception changed for a lot of reasons over decades.

In Nazi Germany gay men were forced to wear a pink triangle on their clothes. Many men avoided pink on their clothes because of it. This is just one very extreme example of the ways we gender color. But it's also a good reason to get rid of gendered ideas around colors or clothes.

This whole chapter can be summarized in just one sentence. Whenever some-one says "Gender is a social construct," they mean:

WE MADE IT ALL UP!

The expectations we have for boys and girls could be the other way around. Or entirely different.

There are no (biological) reasons to assign certain characteristics to one gender.

If gender roles actually were tied to biology they'd look the same all over the world. And they simply don't. Gender always exists in the context of culture and social norms.

In North America a lot of Indigenous communities used to have more than two genders. White colonizers violently suppressed and erased indigenous cultures. (Read more about this in the section "Two Spirit," p. 132.)

Many young people in the Global North find new words to express and explain their gender.

GENDER & THE WORLD

In India, Nepal, Bangladesh, and Pakistan the third option of Hijra exists. Hijra people also use "Kinnar" to describe themselves and often live together in communities.

In a small town in Bolivia, Amarate, gender roles are determined not by biology but by jobs. People there recognize ten different genders.

Do you know other concepts of gender? Which ones do you (not) like? Why?

No matter which social construct we as a society have around gender - we're all taking part in reproducing it. For example...

...by behaving according to a traditional, binary gender role or within society's expectations of our gender.

...when we consume movies, shows, books, and music with the same gender roles.

...when we mock people who express themselves differently than we expect them to.

...by assuming what gender other people have and bringing some unconscious bias into to relationship.

Can you thing of more ways we reproduce gender norms?

> Phew.
> This was quite a lot already, wasn't it. Before we start with the next chapter, here's a super short overview.

WHAT WE'VE SEEN SO FAR:

Biological factors decide which gender we get assigned at birth.

Humans get sorted in two boxes: men and women.

These boxes are full of social and cultural expectations that affect all of us on a daily basis.

What these expectations look like exactly also links back to intersectionality - so race, class, age, religion, or sexual orientation can play a role.
What else do you want to remember from the last chapters?

A BRIEF DIGRESSION ON FEMINISM.

Some people believe feminism means getting rid of gender entirely and making all humans the same. That's not what feminism is about for me.

Things my feminism wants:

* Getting rid of the power imbalance that comes with the social construct of gender.
* Making sure that every person can make their own choices around gender, without being restricted by norms and expectations.
* Justice for all genders on a social, political and economic level.

Your own feminist demands:

4
Gender Identity

Identity is a huge word. And way too complex to fully understand it at this point.

But we also don't have to. Here's a short definition that is enough for the purposes of this book.

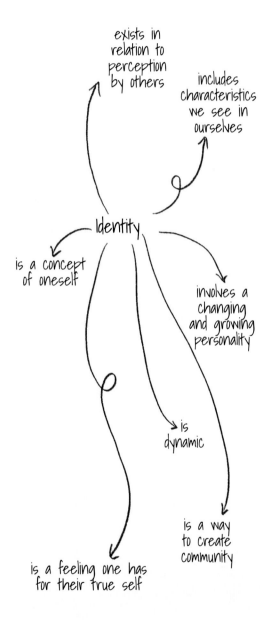

exists in relation to perception by others

includes characteristics we see in ourselves

Identity

is a concept of oneself

involves a changing and growing personality

is dynamic

is a feeling one has for their true self

is a way to create community

What does identity mean in terms of gender?

Gender identity describes your personal, individual, and inner knowledge about your gender.

Our idea about who we are and who we want to be is dependent on the world around us. Religion, family, class, race, sexual orientation, cultural and historic context – all of these are factors when it comes to our identities.

Since the late 2000s more and more people started coming out as trans. But not because suddenly more trans people existed. These people had access to more information, a noticeable fight against the stigma had begun, and being trans became a bit more accepted in society. So the possibility for trans people to come out opened up a little.

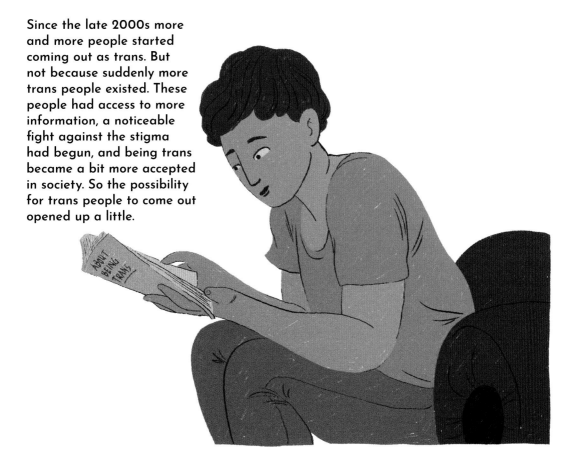

Often we only use the term "gender identity" when we talk about trans people.

"He is a boy."

"He identifies as a boy."

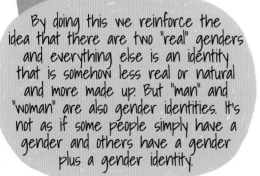

By doing this we reinforce the idea that there are two "real" genders and everything else is an identity that is somehow less real or natural and more made up. But "man" and "woman" are also gender identities. It's not as if some people simply have a gender and others have a gender plus a gender identity.

Figuring out how to speak about gender and using the correct words can feel scary sometimes. Maybe because we don't know how to express certain ideas or we're afraid of making mistakes. Often it is easiest to ask a person which words they feel comfortable with and which ones you should avoid. It's okay to still be learning and to have never heard of some concepts or identities. Take your time — it's a process.

The gender we assign people at birth is based on what we can see of a baby's genitalia. The resulting gender binary is socially constructed and tied to cultural gender roles.

Our gender identity, or just gender, is simply our expertise of ourselves. It's not our bodies or the ideas other people put on us.

Maybe this sounds a bit abstract at first, but it really isn't.

That your gender is a result of your inner knowledge about yourself also means:

You are the expert. You define who you are. Nobody else can (or should) determine your gender but yourself.

Your gender is your truth. No one can take that from you. No gender is more "natural" or "real" than another.

We assume the gender of strangers all the time. But for some people we will get it wrong, because you can't always tell someone's identity just by looking at them. In this book I sometimes use the words "female assumed" or "male assumed." That's one way to express: "I think this person might be a woman/a man, because they fit into my ideas of these gender identities. That doesn't mean, though, that they actually are a woman/a man." We'll explore how expressing and perceiving gender works a bit more in chapter 5.

For many people their gender is just a fact they've never questioned. Some people don't want to identify with any gender. Others question their gender over and over again. All of this is okay.

Figuring out your gender identity can be a bit of a journey and looks different for each person. I will try to tell you some of these stories, as respectfully and lovingly as I can.

There are no wrong ways of handling your gender. You will have to figure out yourself which one feels right for you.

Currently there are two points of view on gender identities that sometimes clash a bit.

On one side, there are people who think gender is only a social construct and power imbalance. As soon as we have deconstructed the social norms there will be no gender left.

One argument for this is: Gender is not a feeling, and your identity construction links back to gender roles and norms.

It's totally fine if you think this way and don't want to identify with any gender. You don't have to relate to the whole idea of gender identities in any way, shape, or form — you make your own choices.

But here's a small comparison. It isn't ideal, but I couldn't think of a better metaphor: If you are not a religious person yourself, it's still not really your place to tell other people they are not allowed to believe in god.

The identities and labels of other people are not less valid if you don't believe in the idea of gender identities.

On the other side are people who believe that gender is part of our identity and gender identities are limitless, because they are so personal.

I sometimes wonder: Don't both sides end up with the same result? Both perspectives are about getting rid of traditional and restrictive gender roles.

If you ask me, there isn't a huge difference between seven billion and zero genders.

To be honest, I don't really care about this debate. Not only because I don't fully get it - what are we arguing about if we all want the same thing? But also because it doesn't change anything about my general approach: I believe that every person has the right to make their own choices - in their perception of gender just as much as their own identity. Respecting other's genders should be a given, no matter what you believe on a more abstract level.

So should we ever find out that gender identity doesn't actually exist and can be deconstructed with gender roles - well, I'd still want to meet people, who do name a gender identity for themselves with respect, kindness, and curiosity.

For this book, this means: I will not discuss or answer these two popular questions.

How many gender identities are there!?..

Is it good or bad that the amount of gender identities is constantly growing??

Instead, I'm trying to share the perspective and experience of different people in this chapter.

I have made this decision because I don't see myself (or anyone really) as being in the position to tell you what gender should mean to you personally. Gender is complicated – yeah, I know, I'm repeating myself – and as long as we as a society are making progress I'm okay with everything still being a bit confusing and messy. Different people choose different paths in life. And I just want everyone to be able to make an educated and empowered choice for themselves.

Some people feel empowered and encouraged by finding the word that describes their gender. It may feel like two pieces of a puzzle clicking together after a long and annoying search. Figuring out which words to use for oneself can be helpful in communicating your emotions and needs.

But maybe labels are just not your thing. That's okay. You don't have to do the whole gender identity labeling thing.

Before we finally dive into different
gender identities, here are a couple of
disclaimers for the next pages.

The list of identities introduced here
is incomplete and always will be. Your
gender is important and valid, even if it
doesn't show up in this book.

This chapter is a bit of an overview of
labels/terms and the identities behind
them. This list is here to explain the
experience of others to you, not to help
you determine the gender of other people in your life.

This list is not a finished or fixed truth.
All these descriptions will never be
perfect, and a lot of the experiences
portrayed are specific and individual
ways of handling gender. The exact
understanding of their gender identity
is still up to every person individually.

Please
don't assume you know
everything about gender
identities that you need to
know after reading this chapter. You don't. I don't. It's fine.
We're all still figuring this
stuff out.

Some of these words might seem interchangeable to you. But the small differences are really important to the people behind these identities. And with most labels comes a community, a history, a form of activism.

On top of that, our attitude toward language changes all the time. The word "queer" used to be a slur, for example. There are still older LGBTQIA+ people out there who don't feel comfortable with that word as a descriptor for their identity, whereas younger people have reclaimed the term and now use it as a positive way to describe their identities.

I'm probably going to say this a couple times more, but anyway: just ask a person what terms they are comfortable with instead of simply sticking a label on them because you think it might fit. That's also a way more relaxed approach for you. Because it means there is zero pressure for you to remember all these labels and identities. This is not about learning a new vocabulary. This is only about treating each other with care and respect.

CISGENDER

If the gender identity of a person aligns with the gender they were assigned at birth, the person is cisgender or just cis.

Cis and trans are words that describe the relationship between one's gender assigned at birth and one's gender identity. For some people being cis or trans is also part of their identity. When it comes to gender and describing your gender specifically there aren't any set rules. Do whatever feels right for you.

Describing other people as cis or trans isn't always appropriate. Who you want to share with whether you're cis or trans is up to you – and this is the same for everyone. We should respect their decisions to only tell a few people, or only family, or no one at all, or everyone. For trans people it can be very uncomfortable or even dangerous if their gender is discussed openly.

It is never okay to out trans people without their consent. But it is important for cis people to acknowledge that being cis or trans shapes your worldview profoundly. These categories exist and they are important and therefore relevant in many conversations.

Cisgender people have it easier in our society in a lot of ways. They don't need to come out. The don't have to explain or justify their gender identity. Most of them don't experience dysphoria. (We will explore what dysphoria is in the next couple of pages. Or you can take a look at the cheat sheet.) A cis person doesn't need to think about transitioning or dealing with restrictive legislation.

These things are part of something called cis privilege. Cis privileges also include representation in media as being the norm. Being the standard in education and medicine. Not having laws made against you. Politicians expecting being cis as the standard. (I could continue this list as cis privileges are so numerous – but I just wanted to give you a glimpse.)

All of this does not mean that cisgender people never struggle with their gender. Cis people also have to deal with gender roles and all the expectations and rules coming with them. To live as a man or women within the gender binary can be super hard, no matter if you're cis or trans. (More on masculinity and femininity on pages 100 and following.)

"Who am I and how do I want to express myself?.."

– a question virtually everyone you know at some point has asked themselves.

TRANSGENDER

"Trans" is an umbrella term for people whose gender identity doesn't align with the gender they were assigned at birth.

The existence of trans people is not a new phenomenon. The trans community has a long history and if you're interested in it, this might be a book for you:

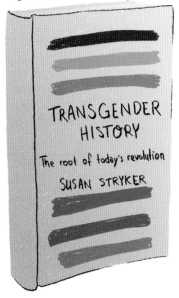

TRANSGENDER HISTORY
The root of today's revolution
SUSAN STRYKER

A lot of trans stories were erased over the decades. Documents no longer exist or never existed. Trans people were pushed to the margins of society for a very long time. Their stories and voices were silenced on purpose.

Today there aren't more trans people than before. They are simply more visible. And more people feel comfortable and safe with discovering, sharing, and naming their gender. We are still fighting the stigma. And visibility often comes with a high price — harassment and threats, for example.

Trans people have always existed and will continue to exist. So everyone might as well just learn to accept it.

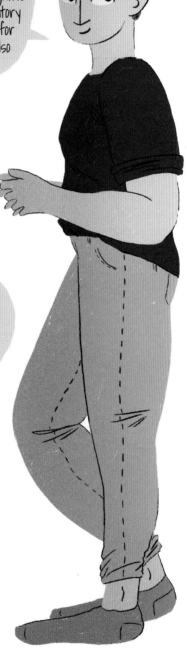

A couple years ago the term used to describe trans people was "transsexual." Today a lot of people don't like that word anymore and think it's a bit old-fashioned. The ending "sexual" implies a connection to biological sex and there doesn't have to be one. Also the term comes with a negative connotation for many as it often was meant in a derogatory way. "Transsexualism" was the official medical diagnosis for trans people, and using a word for an identity that also labels you as "sick" may not feel great.

But there are still people out there who identify as transsexual. Maybe they come from a different generation, or the word is more accpeted by their doctors who have power over their transition, or maybe it just feels right. If someone uses transsexual as a word to describe themself that's totally fine and not old-fashioned.

A lot of people just say "trans" today. Leaving out the ending means holding space for trans people to decide for themselves - transgender, transsexual, or just trans.

Trans identities are not tied to the gender binary. A person can be agender and trans. Or non-binary trans. We'll get to these words in a second. I just wanted to make clear right now: being trans doesn't look the same for every trans person. Not all trans people have the same experiences. Just like cis people, trans folks have their own stories and identities.

When we talk about trans people who are men and women we often say "trans man" or "trans woman." A trans man is a man who was assigned female at birth; a trans woman was assigned male at birth. But their being trans is not a piece of information that everyone needs to have. It is enough to describe a trans man as a man and a trans woman as a woman. (Unless they asked you to do otherwise, of course.)

Other terms you might encounter when learning about trans issues:

FTM is an acronym for "female to male" and describes the transition of becoming a trans man. Some people don't like this term because it implies that a trans man used to be a woman — and there are a lot of trans people who say: "Nope, always was a guy." So there's the alternative MTM, which stands for "male to male." The term clearly states that the gender didn't change while implying a transition at the same time: It's not the identity that changed, but maybe the expression, the way others perceive the person or their social role.

These terms work in the same way as FTM/MTM. MTF stands for "male to female." Again, some people prefer FTF, "female to female."

"Transfeminine" is word to describe someone being assigned male at birth but identifying to some extent female and/or expressing themself in feminine ways. Transfeminine people could for example be trans women, demi women, non-binary transfeminine people, or multigender people.

And of course "transmasculine" describes the same phenomenon "the other way round."

When a person tells you they're trans, you are allowed to ask them which labels and words they feel comfortable with.

A lot of people respond to the whole trans topic with something along the lines of: "Well, I just don't know anyone personally who is trans." First, that doesn't mean you're allowed to not care about trans issues. And more importantly: You can't tell if someone is trans or not just by looking at them. Just because you don't know of anyone in your social bubble being trans doesn't mean that actually nobody is. Maybe they just didn't tell you.

If you want to hear some trans stories, here are a couple of people who speak publicly about transitioning and their experiences with being trans:

Whenever you read up on trans stories please keep in mind that these people are more than trans. Their identities are just as complex and layered as anyone else's. We don't have to "reduce" people to their status as trans person.

Laverne Cox

Thomas Page McBee

Carmen Carrera

Fox Fisher

Annie Wallace

Jack Monroe

How trans people feel will probably never be fully tangible for cis people. Here's a little exercise in empathy that might be helpful for some cis readers.

Imagine the whole world treats you like a man (if you're a woman)/like a woman (if you're a man). You are addressed with a name that's not really yours. People use the wrong pronouns for you all the time. You are expected to behave in ways that are strange to you, and you struggle with your gender role. If you're shopping for clothes people look at you funny if you shop in the section you feel at home in. Can you think of specific moments and imagine being misgendered in them? How does it make you feel? Can you make this feeling bigger? How would your life look like if that feeling was present in your everyday life?

Being cis also means you usually don't really have to fundamentally question your gender; it's just there. That is an option not accessible to trans people.

By the way, there are a couple of studies suggesting that the negative feelings trans people can have around gender are not the result of their being trans; the mental health struggles of trans people are mostly caused by the way society treats trans people. This is just one of the reasons why the WHO (World Health Organization) removed "being trans" from their index of illnesses.

Whenever cis people try to imagine being trans, the phrase "born/trapped in the wrong body" gets thrown around. And while this applies for some trans people, it doesn't for many others. Some trans people only use that explanation to get acceptance from cis people instead debating their identity.

Figuring out you're trans can be a long and exhausting process.

All of us have a sense for who we are. For some people, this self-image doesn't fully align with their body. That feeling is not exclusive to the trans experience.

Some trans people struggle with not fitting into the "born in the wrong body" narrative and question whether they are "trans enough."

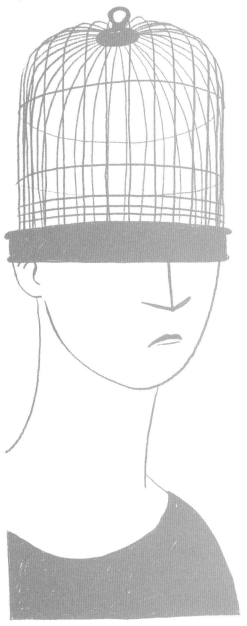

On top of that, our society isn't the most loving and caring toward trans people. So all of us have a bit of transphobia internalized, for example through harmful stereotypes. The thought that being trans is "not normal" is one trans people have to deal with and unlearn as well.

And that's only two reasons why trans people might take a while before they figure out they're trans.

To all the readers currently questioning their gender: Take your time. It's okay not to know immediately. Be patient with yourself; you'll figure it out.

Many trans people find out they're trans through feelings of gender euphoria or dysphoria.

"Gender dysphoria" is a term to describe all the negative, hard, and complicated emotions a person might feel when their gender identity doesn't align with their assigned gender or gender role.

To me, dysphoria feels like there is a connection missing, between body and mind, that everyone around you seems to have. My body is that of a stranger. This body has nothing to do with me. How others look at this body and think it's me makes me angry and sad and overwhelmingly insecure. This body is just not how it's supposed to be.

I compare dysphoria to a map. Every person has a sort of inner map of their body. You can tell where your toes are and how many you have without looking. As a trans person, my body had some errors. It's not that the whole map was off, just some areas didn't fit. These gaps, that's where my dysphoria lies.

Some trans people experience dysphoria mostly in social interactions because they're not seen or treated the way they wish to be.

Others have a lot of dysphoria about their bodies.

Every trans person has a unique experience with dysphoria. And there are trans people who don't experience dysphoria at all - which doesn't make them any less trans!

The opposite of dysphoria is gender euphoria. That is the feeling of joy and happiness if your gender is reaffirmed – either in your self-image or through the way others see you.

My gender euphoria feels like two pieces of a puzzle finally fitting together after a long time of trying. It's a sense of relief and pride. I feel euphoria when others use my name and show me support. I feel euphoria in small situations of everyday life. For example, being able to use the right restroom without anyone making a double-take.

The first time I felt happy and confident in my body was when I wore a binder. I loved the way my clothes fell over a flat chest. I loved the way others looked at me. My immediate thought was: It's supposed to be this way! This is how my body was always meant to look.

Feelings of euphoria and dysphoria vary in intensity for people. Some only experience them temporarily, others long term. A permanent dysphoria can be a painful experience for trans people. It might even lead to depression or anxiety. All the more important to be supportive, caring, and loving with trans people as a cis person!

Many people think I'm just a butch woman. I think about that constantly. Whenever I go shopping for clothes, when I get dressed in the morning, I ask myself: How can I elude the gender binary?

My moments of euphoria are often immediately followed by dysphoria. A child once pointed at me in the supermarket and asked really loudly: "Mom, is this a boy or a girl?" I was so happy. I don't want to be one or the other and the child not being able to tell made me feel whole. But the mother looked at me and answered: "A girl, I believe." My only thought was: Why? This enforced binary makes me sick. I've been in therapy for years, I can't handle this social dysphoria by myself. But as an agender trans person there isn't really a way out of being dysphoric. Sometimes I am jealous of binary trans people and their option of gender reassignment.

Euphoria and dysphoria aren't topics exclusive to trans people. They ended up in this section of the book because it's an issue often raised when we talk about being trans. But I want to make sure that everyone knows: Not every trans person has these experiences and yet they are still trans! Also, trans people aren't the only ones who experience these emotions, and these feelings don't necessarily mean you're trans. Again, your gender identity is something only you can explore, feel, and define.

Many trans people decide in favor of some sort of transition. Again: not to transition doesn't make anyone "less trans." A transition describes all the measures someone can take to minimize dysphoria. This can include social, medical, or legal transitions.

Not all options are accessible to all trans people. For example, legal or financial limitations or health conditions can be a barrier. These people are still trans. A person is not more or less trans depending on how much transition they've gone through.

When people talk about transition, another word that might come up is "passing." It comes from the verb "to pass" and refers to the way other people perceive you. Passing means, for example, that a trans woman is simply seen as a woman by others; she can pass as cis. Being visibly trans can be dangerous and threatening, so passing is an issue of safety for many trans people. For others, passing as cis is not something they want to do.

I'm not able to use a binder to make my chest look flatter because of a health issue. I always wear clothes big enough to hide my chest but still don't feel comfortable. Often I have to explain to other trans men why I'm not wearing a binder before I'm fully accepted as one of them. My therapist, who is supposed to support me, also doesn't fully believe I'm trans – apparently the fact that I'm not willing to risk my physical health shows that my psychological pain isn't big enough. So medical transition is really hard for me to reach.

My transition was a journey to self-love. It's not that I hated my body before. This is my body, this is my home. But I am calmer now, I feel more balanced. I notice a positive effect in my mental health.

When transitioning, many trans people choose a new name and often new pronouns. If someone makes that choice, it is important to respect that choice and start using the new name and pronouns immediately.

Making sure to use the correct name and pronouns is really important. The trans person probably had to have a lot of courage to even share this with you. For them to feel supported and seen, we, as their friends, family, or coworkers, have to respect their needs. And yes, of course we'll be making mistakes along the way. Having known a person under a certain name (also called "deadname") for a long time means that we might use the wrong name by accident sometimes.

If you do make a mistake: Don't apologize over and over again. That just draws an unnecessary amount of attention to the matter. Thank the person who brought up the mistake, apologize, correct yourself, and then move on.
Using the correct names and pronouns is mostly a question of habit. To not try because you're lazy or you feel it's "too complicated" isn't a good reason for not supporting your trans friends. You probably wouldn't like it if someone constantly called you by the wrong name simply because they can't be bothered to remember.

Here are some other aspects of socially transitioning:

Wearing new clothes.

Choosing a new hair-style.

Picking different shoes, accessories, or makeup.

Wearing a binder, which makes your chest look flat. Or beginning to tuck, which creates to illusion of someone having a vulva.

Vocal training.

Accepting oneself and sharing one's own identity with pride.

When it comes to a legal transition, the gender marker and name change are the main focus for a lot of trans people. That includes getting official documents like your birth certificate or ID changed. It could also include things like past diplomas, your driver's license, or your health insurance. To make these changes, trans people have to overcome a lot of barriers. Most countries have legislation in place that makes it very difficult to get these changes made.

But: These changes are really, really important for a lot of trans people.

Consider your name in your contract at work or your certificate of employment, for example. Just imagine the deadname being all over these documents – the trans person then is forced to come out as trans to each potential new employer.

Another example would be teachers or lecturers who refuse to use any other name than the one stated in legal documents. That can make life really hard on trans kids.

The medical transition is all about the decision a trans person makes about their body.

These decisions not only rely on the amount of dysphoria a trans person might experience. They also depend on ...

... the individual needs of the person. Every trans person wants different things for their body (just like every cis person does). There are also trans people who decide against medically transitioning completely.

... the legal options available to a person: is a medical transition even legal where that person lives?

... the financial resources of the person. Does health insurance cover the medical expenses? Who can pay for a surgery if that's not the case or if the trans person doesn't have insurance?

... the individual's personal safety. How much violence against trans people is present in the immediate environment of the trans person?

... the individual's personal network. Does the trans person have enough supportive people in their life, for example to take care of them after surgery?

... the available medical options and risks.

Something called "medical gatekeeping" also plays a huge part in transitioning. This term refers to the idea that a complete stranger is guarding the gate you want to pass through and can determine the conditions under which you're allowed to continue on with your journey. In terms of transitioning, a gatekeeper is any person you have to convince that you're "really trans" or "trans enough" to get access to gender-affirming steps.

Many medical professionals aren't experts on gender or trans people's needs. They still make decisions along the lines of binary gender identities and the norm of heterosexuality. They might expect trans women to wear skirts and makeup. Trans people are often asked to provide proof of their identity: They have to convince these strangers that they are "real" men and women before they can get the medical procedure they want and need.

This process is easiest for white trans people without disabilities who have a stable financial background. For people experiencing different marginalizations (look back on pages 15-17 for a refresher on intersectionality), the gatekeeping might be even harder to overcome.

Part of a medical transition may be hormone replacement therapy, top surgery to create a flat chest or breasts, or bottom surgery to change one's genitalia or reproductive organs. A medical transition can also include things like laser hair removal or lip injections. Measures like these are sometimes called "gender reassignment." Another term is "gender affirmation."

If you meet a trans person, it is incredibly inappropriate to ask about their medical transition. First of all: the person isn't more or less trans depending on the amount of surgery they went through. And second, it's not really any of your business, is it? How often do you ask your cis friends about their genitalia?

I won't list all the possible medical steps a trans person could take. Our health-care system is changing over time, as are medical technologies and access to medical procedures depending on elected government officials. But more importantly: This book is only an introduction. If you think you might be interested in medical transition, you can get more information from trans peers and communities, charities, and trans-friendly medical and mental health professionals. At the end of this book you can find more resources.

"Non-binary" is defined as the negation of something. I prefer "third gender" or just "trans." Just as I am not "not white," I am not defined by the ways I don't fit into your norms. I get to describe my own identity.

When I first started describing myself as a trans man, my dysphoria just exploded through the roof. Being misgendered caused me to have panic attacks. I saw my body as "too feminine" and I self-harmed. I thought I had to feel this way, like I was in the "wrong body." Realizing that I can love parts of this body, my body, and still be trans, is a process. I guess it has a lot to do with internalized transphobia. But it also has to do with internalized sexism. I grew up learning to hate myself.

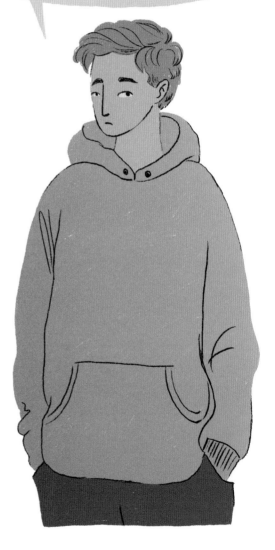

When I was younger I imagined all my problems going away by fitting into mainstream ideas of femininity. I wished for bigger breasts, I wore lace lingerie, I put on makeup every day. I am not the typical trans person who already knew as a kid. I first had to figure out where on the spectrum I feel comfortable. And for the longest time I only considered the "female" options on that spectrum for myself.

Considering hormone replacement therapy to be the "natural" thing to do for all trans people is an incredibly Eurocentric view of things. I get perceived as more masculine than white people do, no matter what I'm doing. Being Black in Germany is associated with similar character traits as being a man in Germany. Even if I walk through the streets in high heels, I'll still be seen as more masculine than your average cute white girl. I don't have to perform masculinity for white people by taking hormones. And my Black siblings don't even get why I would need to.

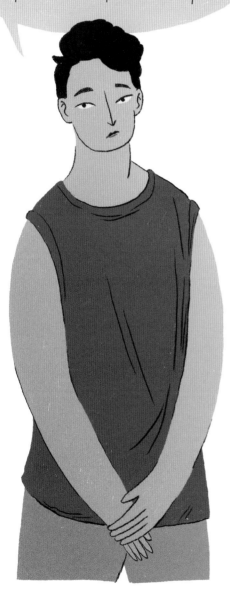

Every now and then you might meet people who don't want to tell you their identity or just don't use any label at all.

Reasons for that could be:

- They are unsure themself.
- They don't know you well enough to trust you.
- They just don't want to tell you.
- Their identity changes too often for any label.
- They feel like a label might limit them in some way.
- They are scared of stereotypes and stigma.
- They don't believe in gender as a part of identity.
- They simply don't want to use a label.

Can you think of more reasons?

All of the above, and any other reason, is completely valid for not using a label or choosing not to share it. Just because some people feel more comfortable when using one doesn't mean everyone has to.

Okay. After all of this talking about identity and cis and trans we are now actually diving in, for real. In case you don't want to read these chronologically or want to skip some descriptions, here's a signpost to guide your way. The next chapter starts on page 167. And just one last quick disclaimer: I included some views and explanations from people with these genders. That doesn't necessarily mean I share their views, myself. Also, none of these people individually speaks for the whole community. This section is meant as a glimpse into all the perspectives and voices within different communities.

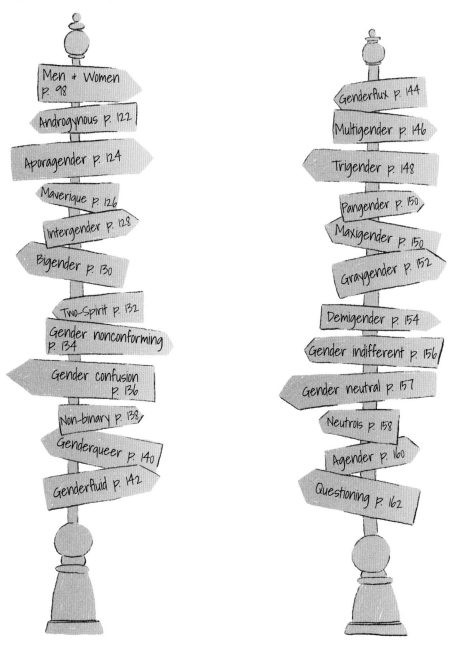

Men & Women p. 98
Androgynous p. 122
Aporagender p. 124
Maverique p. 126
Intergender p. 128
Bigender p. 130
Two-Spirit p. 132
Gender nonconforming p. 134
Gender confusion p. 136
Non-binary p. 138
Genderqueer p. 140
Genderfluid p. 142

Genderflux p. 144
Multigender p. 146
Trigender p. 148
Pangender p. 150
Maxigender p. 150
Graygender p. 152
Demigender p. 154
Gender indifferent p. 156
Gender neutral p. 157
Neutrois p. 158
Agender p. 160
Questioning p. 162

MEN & WOMEN

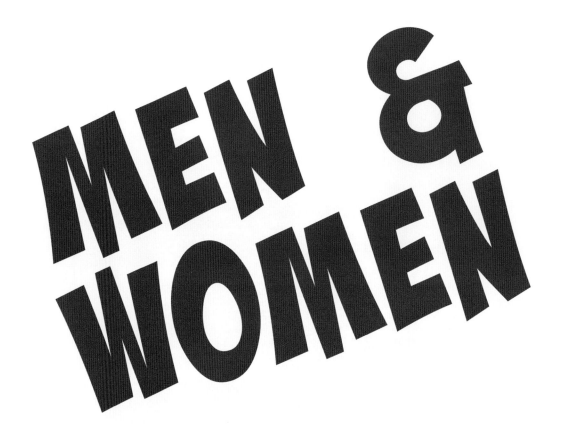

Everything you have to do to be a man/a woman:

The gender you were assigned at birth doesn't matter. Also, the way others perceive you doesn't erase your identity. If you identify a certain way, that is real and valid, and nobody should question it.

Identify as a man/ as a woman.

Done.

MASCULINITY

The most prevalent image of men in our society is one of strength. Men are the providers, men should be in control, men should take on responsibility and not show any weakness.

Men often have difficulties admitting their struggles or problems. For many men it seems impossible to experience, express, or process a wide range of emotions. Suppressed emotions often include sadness, fear, or loneliness. Pushing these emotions to the side leads to mental health and/or anger management issues for some men. But because men are taught not to be "weak," they rarely look for help. Their struggles become visible in high rates of alcohol and drug abuse and suicide.

In general, men have a higher probability (than women) to die early. They are expected to perform more dangerous or physically demanding jobs. They are also more often involved in crime, as perpetrator as well as victim.

When men display emotions typically associated with women or feminity, they sometimes get called a "pussy" or are confronted with homophobic slurs.

This isn't only unfair to men; it is also based on the idea that women and gay men are "weaker" and "inferior."

All of these things are sometimes described with the term "toxic masculinity."

Toxic masculinity doesn't mean that men are toxic or masculinity is something inherently bad.

But this idea of strength, the mindset that men are these cold humans who never cry, who are never afraid or in need of love and support — all this has something destructive about it. And that's what we call toxic.

Some men suffer becasue of their gender role. Or maybe they don't even want to have anything to do with it.

Still, the cold guy only interested in sex and punching people is very prevalent in our society. Many protagonists in big movie productions objectify women, are aggressive and violent, or try to be intimidating and "strong."

These protagonists are also the heroes, though. We watch them saving the world — and might even begin to celebrate their character traits as those of heroes. Oftentimes we don't question critically enough what we're seeing and internalizing.

Some of the characteristics associated with masculinity can be helpful or empowering.

Others will limit your options and keep doors closed for you.

No homo bro.

The biggest problem with our ideas about masculinity? That we expect male assumed people to live up to them! Enjoying ballet and talking about feelings? No way, that's girly stuff. Thoughts like that are harmful. It is not okay that every man showing emotions immediately has to clarify that he isn't gay. (It's also not okay that we apparently still have so much internalized homophobia that we expect men to not be gay!)

Expressing emotions and dealing with them in a healthy way is a really important skill. And it's a skill that will help you grow as a person, regardless of your gender.

This type of masculinity isn't only toxic, it's also very fragile. Maybe you wanted to defend yourself already while reading this. Or tell me that all of this isn't true at all.

Not all men are like this!

What have I ever done to you!?

I personally would never behave in such a way!

Just leave me alone with your feminist agenda. This has nothing to do with me.

Fragile masculinity describes the defense mechanism a lot of people fall into as soon as we start a conversation about male privilege or sexism.

This defense can take different shapes.

Starting an argument.

Anger and aggression.

Staying silent and not participating in the discussion.

Erasing discussions, for example by deleting posts on social media after being criticized for them.

Erasing or not participating in discussions sometimes is described as "male silence."

Remaining silent says a lot. It says: I am okay with the way things are. I am willing to look away while a lot of bad things are happening.

Remaining silent also serves to protect your own privilege and keep the gender binary and its power imbalance alive. And, of course, this behavior isn't exclusive to men.

Just like fragility, silence shows up in different types of behavior — for example by changing the topic as soon as someone so much as whispers the word sexism. Or by justifying your own sexist actions by finding explanations that have nothing to do with gender. Not joining in discussions about discrimination. Not participating in protests for the rights of women and LGBTQIA+ people. Not signing petitions for gender equality. Not sharing posts on social media. Criticizing others for the tone they're using instead of actually listening to what they're saying.

Can you think of more ways a discussion can be interrupted or derailed? Which of those have you used yourself before? With whom? Why?

Fragile masculinity also means that a lot of men like to think of themselves as victims who were viciously attacked by angry feminists as soon as a conversation about masculinity begins.

Oftentimes this destructive behavior comes from a place of fear — fear of an exhausting reflection of oneself or fear of admitting one's own mistakes.

That is not only annoying in conversations, it also ruins your chances of actually listening and learning. Male fragility prevents a lot of men from becoming the great supporters against sexism, homo-, and transphobia they could be.

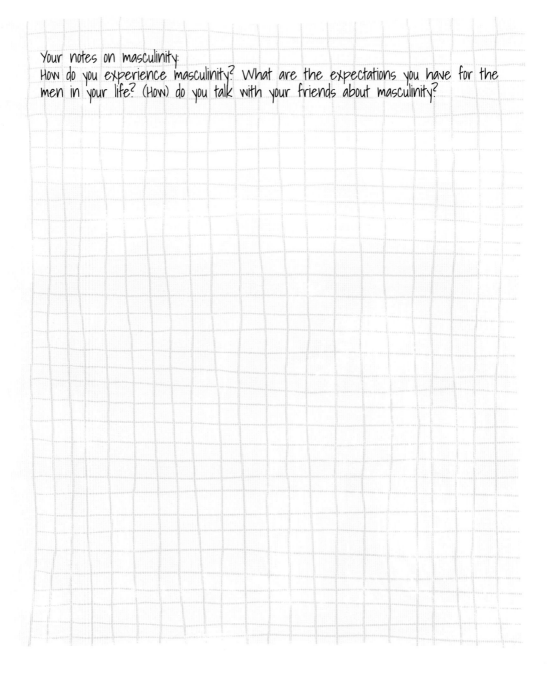

Your notes on masculinity:
How do you experience masculinity? What are the expectations you have for the men in your life? (How) do you talk with your friends about masculinity?

For both masculinity and femininity, it is important to mention intersectionality again. (See pages 15-17 if you need a reminder on what that is.) Gender as a concept has a very racist history. Quick content warning here: I'm going to describe some of it now. Back in the nineteenth century, scientists claimed that only white people can have a binary gender and be proper men and women: white people were deemed to be more "advanced" than BIPOC. Of course, today we know that this is not true! But recognizing the fact that gender is strongly tied to racist ideas and stereotypes is extremely important.

FEMININITY

Our con-
cept of femininity is very
one-dimensional. If you want to
revisit gender roles of womanhood
you can review chapter three,
starting on page 40.

If we only know one story about a group of people, we eventually begin to believe that all members of that group must be as described in that one story. We internalize these stories and they become unconscious bias.

Being raised as a girl means being raised with all of these stories about beautiful, passive, and emotional women. And to some extent, we internalize them and start believing it ourselves.

Here is a real-life example illustrating how much the stories we hear about our own identity affect us. Two groups of students were given some math problems to solve. To one group the scientists supervising the study said: "There were no differences in the performances of boys and girls on previous tests!" The other group heard that girls performed worse than boys in solving these tasks. This announcement had a significant effect on the results. One group showed no gendered performance difference. In the other group, the girls made more mistakes and stated more often that they believed they weren't good at math.

What we tell each other about appropriate gender roles has very real effects. The ideas we reproduce about femininity have the power to shape a whole generation of girls. Our values and patterns of behavior are formed by all this.

How horrifyingly one-dimensional the images about women in our society still are is something we can easily examine with the Bechdel test.

Alison Bechdel came up with this test to determine how well women are represented in movies. The test is simple enough; to pass you only have to answer three questions with "yes."
1. Are there two female characters with names in the movie? 2. Do these two characters ever talk to each other?
3. Are they talking about something other than men?

The test only determines if there is a characterization of women outside of their relationships with men. The test does not look at how well that characterization is done. For example, a movie could portray two women who only talk about lipstick and shopping with each other. And while there is nothing wrong with talking about makeup for hours it still is a superficial portrayal of womanhood.

About half of the movies in mainstream cinema don't pass the Bechdel test. (You can look this up in detail on the website bechdeltest.com.) The other half? Well, that one apparently takes place in a world where women don't exist, or only exist for the pleasure of men. So yeah, it's not really such a weird thing that we have a distorted perception of femininity.

One might think this test has rather low expectations, and that it would be really easy to pass. Sadly, that is not the case.

The Bechdel test does not look at other forms of discrimination. Black women, lesbian women, and disabled women are even less visible on screen than their white, straight colleagues.

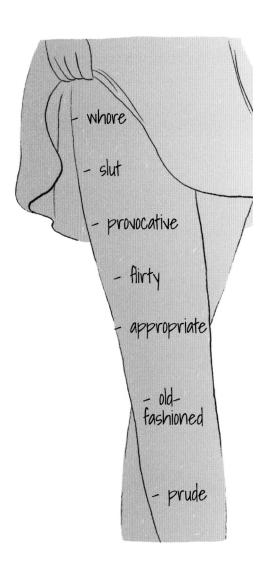

- whore
- slut
- provocative
- flirty
- appropriate
- old-fashioned
- prude

Women often have to walk on a thin line when they try to be feminine in an accepted or so-called appropriate way. For example, they are expected to be "confident" but not "bossy." Or "sexy" but not "slutty." Which of course is nonsense. What even is a "slut"? Women having different sexual partners are not "sluts" and we should stop judging women's sex lives altogether.

This isn't only exhausting but also affects women's mental health.
It is okay if you need help. And it is only courageous of you to look for and accept it.

While men are encouraged to express their emotions in the form of aggression, women are expected to deal with them silently. Many women blame themselves for complicated emotions or negative experiences and often have a bad self-image.

THE NOT-SO-FUN SIDES OF BEING A WOMAN

(Or: Why no one can tell me that we don't need feminism anymore.)

Women have a higher risk for developing eating disorders and unhealthy diets. This isn't because women are weak or easily influenced; the pressure to look a certain way as a woman is just intensely high.

Women have a high rate of developing anxiety disorders and depression. Some studies have shown a connection between these mental health issues and the stress of gender roles.

Governments worldwide are still male-dominated spaces. Laws that affect women are decided by men.

Some women feel like they aren't even their own person. They identify as girlfriend, wife, or mother. The end of a relationship, a divorce, or a child moving out might be especially painful for these women.

Women earn less money than men to this day. Black women and women of color have the lowest pay rates.

Products marketed toward women are on average more expensive than those for men. This is called "pink tax." Women pay a lot of money every year for beauty products and to maintain the physical appearance that is expected of them.

Abortions are still illegal in many countries. And even in places where they are legal, they are often hard to come by. Information is hard to access, and some people have to drive for over 100 miles to find a doctor who will perform an abortion. The stigma the pregnant person might be facing from their partner, friends, and family is an added stressor.

Women have a high risk of experiencing sexual and/or domestic violence and abuse.

We describe certain characteristics differently when we talk about a man versus a woman. This is another result of the double standards we have thanks to gender roles. Here are some examples and some space to add your own:

good leader	-	bossy, too dominant
emotional	-	hysterical, sensitive
gay	-	feminine
handsome	-	pretty
	-	
	-	

These double standards can make it hard for men and women to figure out what their gender identity actually means to them, personally. Here are some ideas how you can respond if you notice any double standards in your everyday life.
- Ask the person what they meant if they said something sexist. Or ask someone to explain a sexist joke. Often the person will notice the double standards themself when questioned about it. And you might avoid the conflict that often comes with speaking up against sexist jokes.
- If you feel up for it: Speak up. Talk to the person. Educate them on why this wasn't okay.
- Talk to your friends on a regular basis about gender. Share your own experiences and expectations. Create space in your friendships where you can experiment with gender and unlearn your double standards without fear of being judged.
- Think about gender when consuming any type of media. Remind yourself that other people don't have to be like these fictional characters.
- Ask yourself every now and then what would happen if you had a different gender. Would you make different decisions? Would you put in the same amount of work to your physical appearance? Would you talk about feelings? What effects do these decisions have on your life? What would change in your life in the long run if you made different decisions now?

All of the things I have written down about femininity and masculinity so far are closely tied to the social construct of gender.

It is important to notice that this construct doesn't just exist as an abstract, separate thing; it is a part of who we are. A lot of us wonder: "Am I normal?" We might even compare men and women to each other and to these norms without noticing.

I am repeating myself here, but this is important: All you have to do to be a man or a woman is to identify as such.

The double standards, the gender roles, the clichés — you don't have to live up to any of it. What femininity/masculinity means to you is for you to explore and figure out. There isn't a right or wrong way to have a gender identity.

Here are some people who told me about their experience with being a woman/a man:

As a boy nobody ever tells you it's wrong to treat others badly. When my behavior made other kids cry the only thing I heard was: Go outside until you calm down. I associate masculinity with a certain disregard toward emotions – others' emotions as well as my own. I don't want to see myself this way. Being a man leaves little room for vulnerability. Being "man enough" means I have to make sure people still see me as strong and powerful. Nobody teaches you that you could be anything, really. Nobody tells you what masculinity really is.

There is extra pressure to be feminine for Black women. Historically and today as well we are never "female enough." We were a tool of white people and white power; they never saw us as real people. We have to overperform femininity to be accepted as women. Long, smooth hair; no visible muscles; tiny, thin, eyebrows that fit the Western beauty standard, and so on. The lighter your skin the better off you are. I know a lot of Black women who bleached their skin and chemically straightened their hair. My femininity isn't mine: white people have too much power over it.

I'd love to say that my performance of femininity is a form of empowerment. I feel strong and confident after putting on lipstick and high heels. But I sometimes wonder – am I just telling myself this because I know I don't really have any other choice? If I show up in my office without makeup my colleagues ask if I'm sick. If I show up to a meeting with unshaved legs people will take me less seriously. Maybe femininity to me means having no alternatives.

I miss male role models. I miss father figures. Since I became a father myself I think a lot about masculinity. What do I want to teach my son? To me being a man means being a good father, a good partner. And that includes wanting to provide for them, financially. I don't see anything wrong with that. But I don't like how little time I get to spend with my child. I miss a lot. When I'm home I try to be really present. Some days that works better than others. My partner only works part-time. It is easy to talk about equality. Before having a child we shared the household chores equally. Now we have to be pragmatic: I earn more money, so I continue to work. She takes care of our son and the household. We don't think this way of doing it is better or worse than other ways. It just made sense for us. I think before we can redefine masculinity we first have to make time for it. Time to be a father, for example.

A lot of trans men get perceived as softer, more emotional, more caring or loving than cis men. And I have no issue with trans men wanting to be more "feminine." But I don't want anyone to tell me I am reproducing toxic masculinity and negative stereotypes because I am not a soft, feminine trans man. I want to go to the gym and watch sports and drink beer. I did these things before transitioning. I think it's problematic that cis people get to decide the acceptable ways of performing gender for trans people.

I hate it when people discuss what's masculine and what's feminine. I hate having to prove myself. Why are some people to obsessed with regulating women's bodies? Other people should not have that kind of power over another person. This is my body. What happens to it should be my free choice. I want to be recognized as a woman the moment I say: I am a woman. Why do people tell me I should have longer hair? Why should I wear makeup? Why should I live by these rules? "Real women" rebelled against them for the longest time – so why put them on me as a condition to accept my identity?

Many people believe that non-binary gender identities have to go hand in hand with an androgynous gender expression. But they don't have to. Honestly, I am sometimes annoyed with how well I fit into that cliché. Trans is an umbrella term and it is a community for such a diverse group of people. Too often, in order to get access to what we need - therapy, a name change, hormones - we have to fit into these clichés. You want to be a trans guy but enjoy makeup? Well, you can just turn around and go back home, nobody will give you the support you crave. I don't know whether I'll forever fit into these androgynous stereotypes. Maybe I will get a sense of empowerment and the courage to experiment with my expression once I get access to testosterone.

I am proud to be a trans woman. It was trans women of color who were so crucial from the start in the fight for the rights of the entire queer community. And this fight is not over. On average a trans person in the US or in Europe lives only thirty-five years. Many trans kids die by suicide because of bullying and hatred. Many trans people of color get killed. We as a society and those of us in the queer community have to rethink what we're doing, radically and urgently. Not every trans person looks trans. Not every trans person will fit into your neat little box of transness. Not every trans person fits your beauty standards. But every trans person deserves respect and support - especially support by white and cis people to tear down the barriers still standing in our way to justice.

I grew up in a neighborhood that some might call a ghetto. Masculinity was always connected to strength. Who was brave enough to steal something from the shop around the corner? Childish tests of courage and boys throwing punches. I had a hard time with that because I always was on the more sensitive and emotional side. Masculinity means a lot of silence, a lot of not talking about feelings. Nobody ever told us but all the boys knew what we weren't allowed to say. We were not allowed to show any weakness, sadness, or fear. These emotions made you less of a man. I still am ashamed for so many of my feelings. And I think that shame comes from the gender role I grew up with. I am trying to unlearn it, but it isn't easy.

Femininity is such an artificial and weird thing. It is expected of women because it makes us into "the other," it marks us as worthless and small. I refuse any kind of femininity. It only turns me into a product of male consumerism. Femininity is a male fantasy, only here to serve male desires and male power. I refuse to paint my face or shave my legs. Men often think I'm lesbian. I'm not. But my body is my tool of resistance. Men know this, so they use laws to restrict and regulate our control over our bodies. To deny us the right to make our own decisions. We still have to fight for the right to define femininity ourselves.

As a man you constantly get told that you have to want sex all the time. Sleeping with a lot of women is kind of a must. But honest conversations around sexuality never take place, especially not during puberty when you'd need them. Other boys in my class told me that I shouldn't be talking about this emotional bullshit, only girls do that. I still believe in this to some extent. My girlfriend and I had a lot of arguments about this when we first got together. There were so many things I never even thought about before. Contraception was a topic that I just viewed as: not my thing, she has to take care of it, just take the pill. I never understood before that her pleasure has to be part of sex. For me sex always was over after I came. I am still learning how to talk about sexuality as a man without being an ass.

I don't really notice my masculinity. Sometimes I'm out with friends in a pub and realize it's only guys. But I don't really care. I don't think I am missing out on something because of it. I have female friends. We talk about different things, that's okay for me. Maybe that's a privilege or something, that I don't have to think about masculinity. I just am one of the guys. You are whoever you are.

I always was a very traditionally feminine girl. Everything had to be pink and glittering and I only played with dolls. Then feminism became a trend. I learned to be confident and that I'd have to be strong to be taken seriously. The new female role models are badass and don't cry. Everything that's too girly is judged harshly as oppressive. I wanted to be strong, confident, and independent. But I also wanted to enjoy girly things. Femininity was always regarded as a sign of weakness, and it still is. I think it's a good thing that feminists are talking about it. My womanhood means: I can enjoy girly things and still demand to be taken seriously.

What is your experience with binary gender identities?

ANDROGYNE

Being androgyne means having an identity that is both male and female or neither male nor female or somewhere between male and female. The word originally meant "both," then "neither." Both meanings are still valid today.

Androgyny describes an ambigious presentation in term of gendered behavior and roles. People of all genders can present as androgynous, some or all of the time. A person who often presents as androgynous might identify as androgyne, or they might identify as something else.

The goal of androgynous people isn't to confuse and provoke cis people or to stand out. Well, maybe it is for some and that's fine by me. But most androgynous people I know just want to be happy and comfortable. If I could ask cis people for one thing it would be this: Stop looking for explanations for the way we are. And stop explaining our existence by centering yourself — this is not about you.

I am female assumed and I am afraid of people just thinking I am a lesbian if I start expressing my gender. I don't want people to make fun of me or think I'm a joke. But even without showing it: I know I am androgyne.

It would be amazing if straight cis men had the courage to explore their androgynous and feminine sides. It is hard to be male and gay - because often the only thing that counts is being gay. We get called names in the street all the time. And we're not a couple but as soon as people see us together they assume we are. Gender needs more freedom. Gender needs to be more playful. And as long as cis men aren't playing, the rest of us will have to live with discrimination.

I wish my body was fully androgynous and just looked how I feel. I wish it was impossible for others to see me as a man or a woman and draw their conclusions. I hate the curves of my body. My bigger breasts, my butt, I'm bothered by it. It took me a long time to realize I am not a trans man. It was important for me to understand gender identities outside of the binary - I am seen and heard here. I feel welcome outside of the binary.

APORAGENDER

The term "aporagender" is a specific identity and an umbrella term at the same time.

As a term, it is used by non-binary people whose gender is fully detached from being male or female or anything in between, and yet they have a strong sense of their individual and specific gender.

To me being aporagender means falling outside of the spectrum but still having a gender. I struggle with describing it as we don't have the words for these feelings and experiences in our binary world. Aporagender is everything that isn't male, female, or agender. Aporagender is its own thing, I feel my gender. Just not the way you'd expect.

I am apor-agender. This label is important to me. It took me a long time to understand who I am. Many people make fun of identities and labels they don't know about. For me it was healing to find a word that describes my identity. I used to feel lost and confused. I couldn't connect with other people because I wasn't connected with myself. When I found my community I found a sense of inner peace and happiness I never knew before. Finally I had a group of people who understood how I'm feeling and who I am.

When I came out many responded with: "Can't I just see you as you? You're the same person, is it really that important?" I know they meant well. But by saying this all these people reaffirmed my feelings of isolation. They suffocated my happiness about figuring out my identity. I thought about this for so long - am I really sure, is this just a phase, do I want others to know? And every time someone says they don't think gender identities are that important or real it is hard for me. I know it is hard to understand an identity that isn't your own. I struggle to understand men. I struggle to understand women. But still I accept that men and women exist. Why can't people do the same for aporagender?

MAVERIQUE

Around the same time the aporagender community was starting to emerge, the term "maverique" was coined. Maverique is another identity that exists for itself, outside and independently of the gender binary.

Aporagender and maverique are similar in meaning. Aporagender can be used as an umbrella term for non-binary identities, whereas with maverique that is less common. Both terms also have their own communities, so they are not interchangeable. For some people it's just about personal preference. For others the difference is really important. And some even use both words to describe their identity.

Let's say masculinity was blue and femininity was red - then maverique would be yellow. It's a color by itself, it cannot be mixed by combining the other two. It has its own hues and variations. For me maverique is citrus yellow.

I think we as a queer community have to stop forming these close connections between our identity and gender or sexual orientation. In my opinion labeling oneself and describing these identities in comparison with a binary experience is utter nonsense. Defining our gender and putting ourselves into a box - why are we doing this to ourselves? I identify as maverique. No other maverique person has the exact same or even similar experience as me. And I think this is true for every gender.

For me being maverqiue has a political dimension: I am in open rebellion against the gender binary. I actively resist the authoritarian attribution of a gender. My gender is determined by my autonomy.

INTERGENDER

An intergender person identifies as between male and female or even as a mix
of male and female. Some people say
intergender is a label that only intersex
people should use, because intergender
describes only their unique experience.
Intersex people don't have to identify
as intergender, though. They can be any
gender.

My identity and story
as an intergender and intersex
person is often ignored or erased. I
constantly have to fight to be seen as
the person I am: someone existing in
the space between male and female. I
understand that other people can feel
like they are between these two gender identities. But being intergender is
more than a feeling, it is about my
body being intersex as well.

Many trans people experience their identities not being taken seriously because they don't have the "right" genitalia for it. That's why I have my issues with making biological aspects a "must have" to be intergender. Gender identities exist beyond bodies. Still, it's neat to have our own thing and be able to make a conscious choice against being sorted into the binary.

There are words that belong only to me. I can call myself N***** and I can call myself hermaphrodite. As a white person, as an endo person, you better not dare to use these words. They are not yours to use. You can't say them without implying that you don't care about decades of oppression and violence and hatred. When a white endo person uses these words I am hurt. I am reminded of trauma. And I don't care what you think of this, this is not about being a snowflake, this is about decency. You can call it political correctness if you want. I call it good manners.

When endo people want to talk about my gender - though I would always question if they really have to - they can use the word "intergender." I am not taking anything from them by claiming some words for myself. I am not shutting down the conversation, I'm just explaining that there are enough alternative words. Use them.

BIGENDER

A person with two gender identities is bigender.

These two genders can be "man" and "woman" or two other gender identities.

Some bigender people experience their genders simultaneously, whereas others experience them in an alternating way. For most the gender experience isn't split evenly. Instead, they experience the two identities with different intensities.

Although bigender and bisexuality often get compared with each other, gender identity and sexual orientation aren't necessarily connected. Comparisons can help us grasp a new concept. But we also have to remind ourselves when using analogies that similarities don't mean the things being compared are the same.

Whenever someone doesn't understand what bigender means I ask them whether they understand bisexuality. Most do and I can use that. My comparison is: I am bisexual in my gender identity. That does not mean I am half woman and half man. It means I sometimes am a woman and sometimes a man, sometimes more, sometimes less.

So many people ask me: "How do you know that you're maverique AND a woman?" I think that is a really strange question. How do you know that you're only a woman? Exactly, you just know. But as long as a person is cis nobody asks them: How do you know? Are you really sure? Can you describe it? I don't think I have to prove anything. I experience femininity — I am not detached from being female assumed... And at the same time I know there is more. Why are so many cis people bothered by me having two gender identities? I don't have to decide. I know who I am and that is enough for me.

I can be a boy for months and then agender for days. I can be a boy for a week and then have a strong sense of being agender for ages. Nobody other than me needs to understand that. Others just have to respect it and keep their opinions to themselves. Especially if they don't believe being bigender is a real thing.

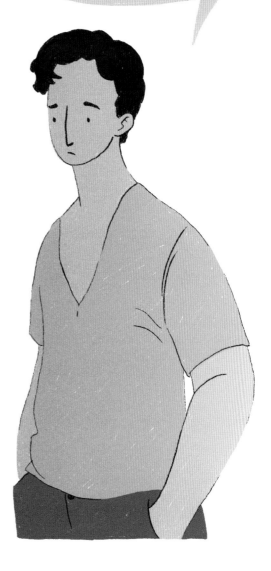

TWO SPIRIT

The term "Two Spirit" was introduced in the 1990s - but the concept behind that name was a lived experience for Indigenous people in North America for a long time before that. The exact meaning of the term is specific to each Indigenous community. "Two Spirit" was a name agreed on by the Indigenous community so that they could have a shared language and a way to educate others about their culture.

As a white person, I have no power over that word. It is not my place to define it. I want to emphasize here that I am only writing down what I read, learned, and heard my-self - this is not about writing down one objective truth. I in no way want to imply that I know everything. Gender and race as categories intersect in many different ways and it is important to me that we remind ourselves of that on a regular basis.

1990 The third annual First Nations gay and lesbian conference took place in 1990. The term "Two Spirit" was introduced and voted on there. It was meant as an umbrella term for different Indigenous gender identities. Toronto Pflag defines the word like this: "Two Spirit refers to another gender role believed to be common among most, if not all, first people of Turtle Island, one that has a proper and accepted place within native societies. This acceptance was rooted in the spiritual teachings that say all life is sacred."[2]

[2] https://www.torontopflag.org/two-spirit

Two Spirit is lived differently in different communities.

In Lakota there is a word, "wínjkte," that can be roughly translated as "to be as a woman" and refers to transcending gender boundaries in ways white people would describe as mtf.

In Diné the word "nádleehi" means "those who transform." It describes the existence of four genders — masculine feminine, masculine masculine, feminine masculine, feminine feminine.

These are only two examples, but there are many more.

Every Indigenous community has their own belief system around sexuality and gender, often tied to spirituality. In many communities, Two Spirit people took on important roles in society — for example counseling couples, being a medical professional, or being a warrior. Two Spirit can include many aspects of gender, sexuality, and spirituality. The term is a wide concept for people with a feminine and masculine spirit.

Two Spirit as a term became necessary because many words used previously were introduced and determined by European colonialists. These words were often meant in a negative and derogatory way. Introducing the term Two Spirit was also about reclaiming power.

European colonization brought with it restrictive gender roles and homophobia. These ideas of "civilization" were violently enforced in Indigenous communities.

Indigenous people were robbed of their land and their spiritual practices and traditions. In many US states, Two Spirit communities were criminalized.

The term Two Spirit is connected to the history of colonialism. It is connected to surviving violence and marginalization. So it's not a term a non-Indigenous person should ever use to describe their identity.

Being Two Spirit can't be experienced by colonialists. The meaning is uniquely ours, it depends on our tribe, our eldest. The term is sort of a blank page. We created it specifically to have a space for our experiences. Each interpretation of Two Spirit is important and none of them is better than another. We don't negate each other.

GENDER NONCONFORMING / GENDER DIVERSE / GENDER VARIANT / GENDER EXPANSIVE

All of these words are umbrella terms people use to describe experiences outside of binary gender norms.

"Gender variant" is a less popular term among them as it implies being cisgender as the norm someone varies from.

These words can be used to describe identities. More often they are used to describe a gender expression. A cis woman who expresses as tomboy could, for example, be described as gender nonconforming. Likewise, a genderqueer person could identify as gender diverse. These decisions are personal and there are no strict rules anyone has to follow.

Gender nonconforming, GNC for short, is about expression. It is important to me to separate GNC from being non-binary. Non-binary is my identify, that's who I am. GNC is how I show myself to the world. Not all queer people are GNC. Non-binary people can just as easily be masculine, feminine, or androgynous. I am not non-binary because I made certain decisions about my outer appearance. GNC men and women are still men and women.

How I express my gender didn't change when I stopped identifying as transmasculine and started identifying as gender nonconforming woman. What did change: I feel strong instead of ashamed and confused. It was important for me to try on the label trans to figure out who I am not. I was tense and afraid my whole life. I was worried about how others see me, whether I am "trans enough," if I look too much like a woman. I tiptoed around my own identity. To describe myself as a GNC woman felt liberating. I regained power over my own body. The label "transmasculine" was important for my survival. It allowed me to transcend boundaries of the gender binary. The words GNC woman and butch help me to define my gender however I want to.

Sometimes I feel like my identity is best described by the reactions of others. "Boy or girl? You can't have it both ways. Pick one or we'll pick for you. Don't forget to perform your gender-choice please. Dress more appropriately. Boys don't wear makeup. Cut your hair or you'll look like a girl. Why are you in the kitchen, your sister can do that. Wash your face, you should know better. Stop crying. Why are you interested in this? Are you trying to be a girl? Why do you dress like that? Change your hairstyle, your clothes, your interest, your personality. You're not gay, are you? I don't understand you. Why are you angry now? Can't you just be yourself? Wait. Not like that."

GENDER CONFUSION / GENDERFUCK / GENDERPUNK

People who intentionally and happily cause confusion around their gender sometimes use these words. Maybe they want to make a statement about gender norms and roles. Others enjoy confusion because they want to start a conversation. And some just feel comfortable when their gender is expressed in ambiguous ways to reflect how complex and confusing it can be at times.

I am not okay with the gender that was assigned to me. I get my confidence by determining my gender, my expression, and my identity by myself. I never identified as trans, as I never experienced dysphoria and have no need for a transition. Genderpunk is a good word for me, because it doesn't take up any queer space where I don't belong. I am not queer. I am a straight cis woman. I will not stop using the label woman, for political reasons. But I refuse to be just that. I am a woman and I am cis-genderpunk.

Honestly, I don't care if people get annoyed. So what if they say we're a bunch of snowflakes trying to get attention. If they aren't enraged about us "trans trenders" they're angry about something else. Young people never get taken seriously. I don't have an issue with conservative old guys being irritated by my existence. I'm irritated by them too.

I like it when people in the street stop and stare at me. I know exactly why they are doing it. Every now and then someone comes up to me and asks: "Sorry, are you a boy or a girl?" Sure, sometimes it's too much, but mostly I like it. I want them to rethink their perception of gender, I want them to feel provoked. I want to bend the rules of gender purely by existing.

You can't decide for others whether their identity is real or not. We will continue to exist, regardless of your opinion.. If you're not supporting all queer people, you're not truly supporting queer people at all. Accepting trans folks can't be tied to your personal conditions or passing in the gender binary.

NON-BINARY

Non-binary is a specific gender identity as well as an umbrella term for identities outside the binary. Some non-binary people use the word "enby" as abbreviation.

A non-binary person could be someone who is neither man nor woman. Or a person having multiple gender identities. Or their own understanding of their identity. The idea of gender identities outside of the gender binary isn't new. Historically speaking, non-binary gender identities always existed; what changed is the language around it and the visibility.

Navigating this world as a non-binary person is a constant struggle. Which restroom do you use? How are you dealing with the gendered security check at airports? How can you find therapists or doctors who respect your identity and make you feel safe? (All of these are issues for binary trans people as well! Want to learn more? Just look up the gendered airport security check issue.)

Many non-binary and genderqueer people suffer under the gender binary. This can lead to mental health problems and a constant questioning of one's own identity.

My community is erased or ignored in this society. Most people just aren't aware of our existence and therefore keep gendering us as boys and girls. I am exhausted by getting misgendered all the time. I often feel invisible and misunderstood. I wish it was different.

The stereotypes, prejudice, and clichés cis people have of us are not important. They do not reflect our lived reality. None of us has to act certain ways to be a "real" non-binary person. I think a lot of non-binary people have a complicated relationship with their own gender. We have to deal with our own insecurities and questions - and then cis people start talking over us and explaining to us how non-binary should look and feel. That's just not okay.

Every non-binary person is different and I want more diversity in our representation. I see a lot of non-binary folks distancing themselves from gender completely. I don't see a lot of non-binary people who have multiple genders or continue to identify with their gender assigned at birth. For me there is no contradiction in being non-binary and a man. My experience with masculinity overlaps with my identity as non-binary. I continue to present male; I am male-assumed and that is a big part of my male identity. Still, I am allowed to have a bigger identity than male. Manhood is my lived experience, non-binary my identity.

When cis people ask me how it feels to be non-binary I compare it to using my non-dominant hand. I am right-handed, so whenever I take a pencil in my left hand that feels uncomfortable and wrong, I don't write as well as I could. It feels something like that when I get misgendered: uncomfortable, it's not the right fit. If I am seen and accepted as non-binary it's like writing with my right hand - an easy flow, I don't even have to think about it.

GENDERQUEER

"Genderqueer," like so many other terms, can either mean a specific identity or be an umbrella term. Some people say genderqueer is the umbrella term for all queer gender identities. It was the most commonly used umbrella term until the early 2010s; then a switch to "non-binary" happened. That shift in language may have to do with finding words cis people accept. So while some people are happy with umbrella "non-binary" others strongly prefer using "genderqueer."

In the 1990s activists who weren't straight were sometimes described as "orientation queer." Inter and trans activists were described as "genderqueer." The definition for genderqueer people expanded over time and started including all kinds of people who break the rules of gender.

"Queer" used to be a slur but was reclaimed and is now used by many in a positive way.

My femininity is queer. I express femme, I am lesbian, a lot of things about me say: Woman. And yet, that's not exactly true. But I don't have to explain or show my queerness. My queerness is inside me, is part of me, is me. I am a genderqueer woman. You can believe me or not – your ability to understand my gender doesn't change anything about its existence.

Before and during my transition I was so sure I am a man. Access to transitioning allowed me to explore queer and non-binary aspects of my gender identity. Am I really a man? Who knows. I am not a woman, that much I know. Now that I've reached a point of being male-assumed, I feel less pressure to fit into the binary. I don't have to box myself in anymore just to convince doctors and lawyers. I think this is where my freedom begins.

I hate other people not taking genderqueer seriously as an identity. Yes, it is an umbrella term and yes, it is a description. But it is also my identity. I have dysphoria as a genderqueer person and I get uncomfortable when people use my deadname or wrong pronouns. When I came out my friends said they'd support me and all that. But they still use my old name. "You're not trans, so it's not that bad." - Well, for me it is bad. I am not binary trans, I know. But still, I deserve some respect.

GENDERFLUID

People who are genderfluid have a gender identity that is always or often changing. The identity might shift between one gender at a time or take shape as several identities at once. Some genderfluid people experience a change at random moments; for others there are specific triggers for a change.

The way cis people talk about identities like genderfluid has an impact. Cis people too often dominate the public debate. Others, including me, fall for it. I didn't want to be genderfluid for the longest time. I thought: What nonsense. Even today I sometimes doubt myself – Am I imagining things? Do all people feel like this? Am I just trying to be special? Having to reaffirm one's own gender over and over again is exhausting. I am trying to balance internalized sexism, transphobia, and a cis-normative view of the world, all while trying to be true to myself. The world desperately needs to change in regard to queer issues.

I find it hard to reach any sort of goal with my gender identity and expression because nobody can teach me how to do both. How can I express and present myself in masculine ways with all this hair on my head but none in my face? How can I remain feminine after starting a transition? I wish I could change my gender like a sweater. Two binary sweaters and I get to decide on a daily basis which one fits better for that day. At the moment I am only myself half of the time and I am devastated by it.

I read this description somewhere and it stuck with me: My gender is a speedometer. A needle that sometimes kicks up to levels of masculinity and sometimes remains steadily in my assigned femininity. Often I'm somewhere in between. I don't choose. I can't just make a left into manhood the way I could on a highway. I just suddenly find myself here, in the fast lane, and I notice it because I experience dysphoria. It's a bit like speeding up but not being able to switch gears or use the brakes. Sometimes this gives me a lot of anxiety and I panic.

GENDERFLUX

A genderflux person experiences their identity at different intensities. Their gender "fluctuates," for lack of a better word. For example, the person might strongly identify as a man one day but feel more disconnected from masculinity on other days.

To my genderflux siblings: This world is an ignorant place. Many people do not understand us; they don't want to try and therefore they ignore us. There always will be moments when we get seen and accepted for who we are and those moments feel great. But currently we can't expect that from everybody. And yes, that sucks. But all we can do about it is stay calm and talk to people, educate them. And most importantly, become visible. We have to refuse to get pushed to the side. Especially by those who don't believe we exist. Continuing to exist and being our wonderful selves is the best way to fight the cis-tem. Stay true to yourself without ever apologizing for it. Cut your hair if you want to. Wear a binder. Wear a dress or a shirt or both. Put the pride flag around your shoulders like a superhero's cape. Make you own pronoun pins. Let people in on your identity, be proud of your identity, and don't let anyone silence you. It will take a lot of time and courage and energy. But together we can achieve radical queer acceptance. We are real, we are valid, and being genderflux is a magical gender identity.

Sometimes I have to laugh out loud about the crap cis people say about gender. When I adjust my expression while being more female I have to deal with people telling me I shouldn't uphold these old-fashioned gender norms. When I change my gender expression people claim I'm making all this up. After I had one expression for a while and adjusted, because my sense of connection to gender shifted, people told me I'm just pretending to be queer. I can't win in these discussions. It's taking up all of my energy to constantly have to justify myself. I don't want to hear these comments. I just want to be more female on some days and less on others.

I am genderflux maverique. Sometimes I have a very clear understanding of my own gender. Other times I can barely grasp it myself. It's a bit like riding a bike. Some days you'll be on autopilot and you know the way without even thinking about it. Other days you feel every damn push on the pedal and have to work harder.

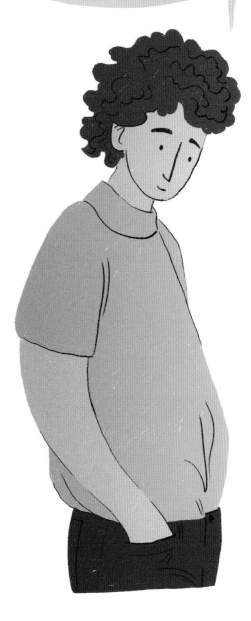

MULTI-/POLYGENDER

A person experiencing multiple gender identities might describe themselves as multigender or polygender. Some people who don't know how many identities they have or who feel like their identity changes over time use that term as well.

My concept of polygender could be described like this: I have many gender identities, but not all of them. For a while I just used "not male" as a descriptor, but I don't want to be defined by what I am not. I have an identity that might be everything but male. Female is definitely included, but my identity isn't limited to that.

I use multigender to describe that my gender changed and that change will always be part of my identity. As AFAB person I experienced sexism. I lived through my childhood and puberty presenting as female. These experiences shaped me and will forever be part of me. I don't want to erase or ignore that. Today I am non-binary trans and multigender. My femininity is still part of my transness. I can't separate that. I have more experience with gender than cis people.

Using identity descriptors is so interesting. How many words do you pick? I see many multigender people being very specific with their identitiy. Cis people get easily confused. They are used to people being able to describe their identity in one word - man or woman. Many reject me when I say that: I am a multigender genderflux non-binary person. I always hope their rejection comes from a place of insecurity and not from bad intentions. It does make me sad though, how often people ex-press their insecurity by judging me.

I don't have any energy left for discussions about how many gender identi-ties one person is allowed to have. Even some queer people claim that a person can't possibly experience more than two or three gender identities. This way of thinking is so deep-ly rooted in the gender binary. We have to move forward from this idea of gender being something we can count. Binary ideas of gender descriptions - no matter how many we come up with - will not liberate us.

TRIGENDER

A person experiencing three gender identities is trigender. These identities can be binary and/or non-binary. Some trigender people experience their three gender identities simultaneously, others in an alternating fashion. Many trigender people don't have three equally important gender identities; instead, their genders can be experienced in different intensities.

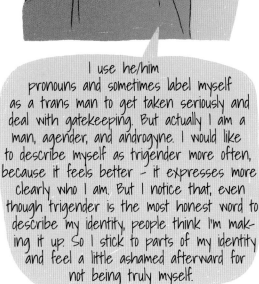

I use he/him pronouns and sometimes label myself as a trans man to get taken seriously and deal with gatekeeping. But actually I am a man, agender, and androgyne. I would like to describe myself as trigender more often, because it feels better – it expresses more clearly who I am. But I notice that, even though trigender is the most honest word to describe my identity, people think I'm making it up. So I stick to parts of my identity and feel a little ashamed afterward for not being truly myself.

Just as easily as you have one gender, I have three. Having only one gender is a very restrictive and suffocating idea to me. If I had to decide I honestly don't know how I'd choose. I experience all of my identities at the same time. And to me that is not overwhelming, but freeing and beautiful.

PAN-/OMNIGENDER

Pan-/omnigender people experience many and sometimes all of the gender identities, either in an alternating way or simultaneously. Many people identifying as pan-/omnigender do so because our current knowledge of gender is limited and they have to assume that there are gender identities that we can't yet describe. Or that our knowledge will change with the fall of the gender binary.

MAXIGENDER

The label "pan-/omnigender" can be problematic. Some gender identities are tied to specific cultural and historic contexts. And maybe it's not the best idea to claim these identities if you're not part of these communities. For example a lot of Indigenous people say that white people shouldn't use Two Spirit as a label.

Therefore people came up with the term maxigender. Maxigender people experience many and sometimes all gender identities accessible to them. "Accessible" means everything wihtin that person's individual context as well as our general knowledge about gender as a society.

I am pangender and I disagree with people trying to take away my identity by claiming political correctness. Most times it is masked transphobia. As if more people would accept me if I started saying maxigender. Whether a label is the politically correct choice for me, is for me to determine. Strictly being against the word pangender means putting me into a position were I have to come out as inter and Indigenous immediately. Educating people about the exact meaning of terms is all good, but we should never end up banning certain identities.

There are so many parts of my identity I can summarize with maxigender. I am genderfluid and I often see myself as genderqueer. They play together in a way and I identify as maxigender because that describes the intersection of the other two best. My gender has four areas: male, female, neutral, and nothing. I feel like all four, and I fluctuate between them. The intensity sometimes surprises me as well. I have many gender identities and I can feel them all.

There isn't a limit on how many identities a person can have. I notice my gender constantly changing and growing. My gender is like a line moving forward, changing shape, changing direction. I keep discovering new aspects about myself, I can't put a number on that. I can't describe all of my feelings in words. So I simply use maxigender: I feel the maximum of gender I can imagine feeling in this very moment.

GRAYGENDER

The term "graygender" describes feeling only a weak connection to one's gender identity and/or feeling a bit indifferent about it. Graygender people do have a gender but they often feel disconnected from it or don't have any interest in it.

I am AMAB and I am okay with being male assumed. It wasn't always like that. In my childhood I always considered myself "not fully a boy" or "nearly a girl." "Man" to me is a label I had to get used to. I first had to realize that I don't have to be traditionally masculine. Still, I don't feel fully comfortable in male dominated spaces. Public toilets for example or changing rooms in the gym. I feel like an intruder. I don't belong there and it's weird that nobody other than me notices. I wouldn't voluntarily go into a group that is "just for men", because I don't feel like I'm part of that.

I identify outside of the binary. I identify with gender, to some extent. There is a natural ambivalence. My need for gender isn't that strong. Graygender is like the smoke after you blow out a candle: It's there, somehow visible, a smell, a feeling. But you can't really grasp it and the moment you try to it's gone.

Most queer people are so colorful all the time. It starts with the pride flag, so many colors. Graygender describes me really well. I am queer, I exist outside the gender binary, but not that intensely. As if someone turned down the saturation in photo editing. There are still colors, but they don't really matter that much.

DEMIGENDER

Demigender can be used in different ways: demiboy, demigirl, demi non-binary, demi-agender. Depending on the combination the meaning changes. In the end it's about a person only identifying in parts with the named gender. "In parts" can mean different things: some demigender people still have a clear sense of their identity, while others feel more detached from gender.

"Demi" is a prefix that often get's "what?" as a response. Then you explain. And then they say: "You're just looking for attention," or: "Why do you need a label for that, just say boy or girl." Explaining one's identity is never easy. Finding the right words to do so is hard. Demigender isn't a label that's widely known or very popular. So I'm not surprised when other people don't immediately believe we exist. But it is real. And every gender deserves respect. Having a label to describe my identity, that is really important to me - it helps to understand myself, to express myself, to build a community and confidence. Nobody has the right to take away a label like demigender just because they are unfamiliar with it.

Being demigirl to me means experiencing femininity in phases. A part of me wants to wear pink dresses and violet lipstick and huge earrings. Another part of me feels strange and out of place when I am surrounded by women - as if I wouldn't truly belong there. I am not gender nonconforming or non-binary. Often I am quite comfortable with femininity, especially the stereotypical ways to be feminine. I sometimes compare it to swimming. You are in the middle of a lake, everything's normal. Then you take a dive and your whole world changes - you feel different, you see, taste, and hear differently, everything around you has changed. But then you come back up and everything is exactly as before and nobody even noticed you just went from one world to another and back.

Maybe I identify as demiboy because I am measuring myself against toxic masculinity. That might be true. Doesn't make it less important. I don't feel connected with that type of masculinity. I only rarely feel like a man. I don't mean to distance myself from gender expression and gender perception by saying that. "I don't see gender" is just as much of a lie as "I don't see race." Demiguy describes my inner self. I am soft and gentle and I startle when confronted with masculinity. I only sometimes can deal with my gender.

GENDER INDIFFERENT

A person who is indifferent about or not interested in their own gender can be described as gender indifferent.

I am okay with being called female, male, agender, bigender, trigender, or anything really. I am not bothered by any of these words. Call me whatever you like, I honestly do not care. But it is not like I am female, male, agender, bigender, or trigender. Because that would mean I have a preference. And I simply don't.

GENDERNEUTRAL

Genderneutral people have a gender identity, but their identity is neutral. For some that means being exactly in the middle between masculinity and femininity. Others say their identity doesn't even appear on the spectrum.

Boobs don't have a gender. Hair color doesn't have gender. Hair length doesn't have a gender. Makeup has no gender. Gender neutral and non-binary people aren't only the skinny people with a flat chest and short, colorful hair you see on Instagram. Expression is not the same as identity. There is no expression that is neutral, but I can still be gender neutral.

NEUTROIS

Neutrois is a neutral gender, often described with the number zero.

Some people who are neutrois experience dysphoria and wish to transition to be perceived in a more gender-neutral way. The urge to transition is not present for all neutrois people though.

There is a connection lacking between the gender I was assigned and what I feel in my truest, deepest self. My consciousness isn't male or female, it's just neutral. I just want to be a person, a human being.

I am so frustrated being stuck in a society that genders everything. It is so hard if you are never truly a part of that. Why should I transition if it's not about my body? How should I achieve neutrality? Gender feels like a circus to me, none of it is real. When I was younger I thought gender was a giant joke and I was the only one not getting it. I thought everyone was making it up. Today I know I have a space in this society as neutrois. But how people view my body as feminine bothers me. My body shouldn't be in contradiction to how I feel on the inside. My gender is mine to determine and I don't have to adjust my body for the cis-normative gaze.

I want to start taking hormones, but my therapist isn't supportive. I'd like to change therapists, but it's not that easy. This therapist was recommended to me by trans people. He's supportive of people feeling trapped in the wrong body. But he does not believe me when I say my gender is null. He says I wouldn't feel better with hormones because a thing like neutrality doesn't exist in this world. I just want to decide for myself how I express.

As girl I learned how to make myself small. I crossed my legs and folded my hands, shoulders back, never taking up too much space. I was everything expected of me. Did I do it wrong? Maybe. My teenage self still wonders: Shouldn't I have been a wild child, one climbing up trees and having blood on my knees from falling down in a jungle gym? Could tomboy have been my identity? My vocabulary used to end with the boundaries of my village. My accent doesn't match the big city, but I'm learning new words here and feel taller. That's called code switching but code switching is not a term understood in my home. I turned inward. I found a strong and soft core inside myself. I forgot and ignored and made myself smaller. At some point I was so small that I became nothing. How long did I shrink? Where is that tension coming from? Does it have to be this way? What happens if I start taking up space? How does it feel to breathe freely?
I have blood on my knees and cross my legs. I fold my hands into one another while sitting in trees. I'm not making myself small since I don't have to be the cute girl next door anymore.

AGENDER / GENDERLESS / GENDERBLANK / GENDERFREE / GENDERNULL / GENDERVOID

Some people use all of these words interchangeably. To others the nuances are super important.

Some people identifying with these terms feel like they don't have a gender identity. Others describe it more as a neutral gender. Some people identify like this because they reject the concept of gender or consider it irrelevant to them personally.

Realizing that I reject womanhood, not only femininity, was a moment that fundamentally changed my life. I feel much more comfortable since I discovered the word genderless. I am not a tomboy or an androgynous woman, all of that felt only partially right. I refuse gender. I am not only refusing gender, I am distancing myself from it. Fully intentionally and without giving anyone a say in it.

Sometimes I forget that gender exists. When I'm surrounded by other agender people and friends, where I'm out. Then I go outside and strangers suddenly gender me and I am surprised by it, more than I should be.

Genderfree doesn't mean androgynous. A lot of people confuse these things or believe only androgynous people can truly be genderfree. Sometimes I am more masculine, sometimes more feminine, sometimes something else. That I am genderfree doesn't mean I don't express myself anymore. That others perceive that expression as a gender identity isn't my problem, that's in their own heads. They have to work on their ideas of the world, not me or my gender.

A void is exactly what I feel when I think about my own gender. Being agender comes in a spectrum, just like all the other gender identities as well. I know agender people who don't want to identify with a gender and those who simply don't have one. I describe my gender as a sense of nothing. I can't explain it any better - How are you supposed to explain something that isn't there? Gendervoid as a metaphor already works quite well.

QUESTIONING

"Questioning" is the word people use who are still in the process of figuring out their gender identity. Some people who are questioning might suspect they are trans. Others are still figuring out the label that works for them. And it always is an option to come to the conclusion that you're cis after all.

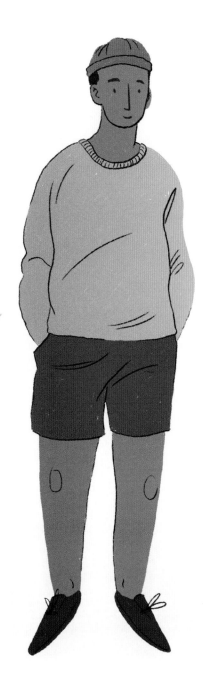

When I stopped wearing dresses and makeup I didn't know I was trans. I only knew that that was how I felt comfortable and that was enough. When I cut my hair I didn't know I was trans. I had a suspicion, but mostly I knew that shorter hair would make me happy, so I cut it. My name and pronouns changed when I used "questioning" to describe myself. That's also when I started wearing a binder. What I'm trying to say is: It's okay to be unsure. It's okay to question your gender while already transitioning. You don't have to have it all figured out to understand what feels right in your gut.

I think it's okay to not be able to define your own gender. I am still myself, even if I can't find a label that works for me. My gender does not define me as a person. I found my peace with this topic while still having questions and still being unsure. I am still getting to know my gender identity, but I don't let that stop me from living my life.

In my opinion many people in the queer community are afraid of uncertainty.. There is so much pressure from the outside. "Not trans enough," "not queer enough," "bisexual people just haven't made up their mind yet," and so on. I have been labeling myself as questioning now for about two years and I like it that way. I think embracing uncertainty is courageous. I don't know where my questions will lead me. Maybe nowhere. That's also fine. Questioning is a wonderful label full of potential and it offers me a lot of room to get to know myself.

What I would have liked to hear while questioning: Relax. There will always be people who love and support you, no matter what will happen. You still have your whole life to figure this out. You are brave and strong and these questions, they don't define everything you are.

Every person you saw in this chapter got three questions from me. Now I am asking you the same:

1. What label do you use for your gender and how would you describe your gender identity, how does it feel, and how do you know you have that gender?

2. What do you want everyone with different gender identities from yours to know about your experience?

3. What would you like to tell people with the same gender identity as yours?

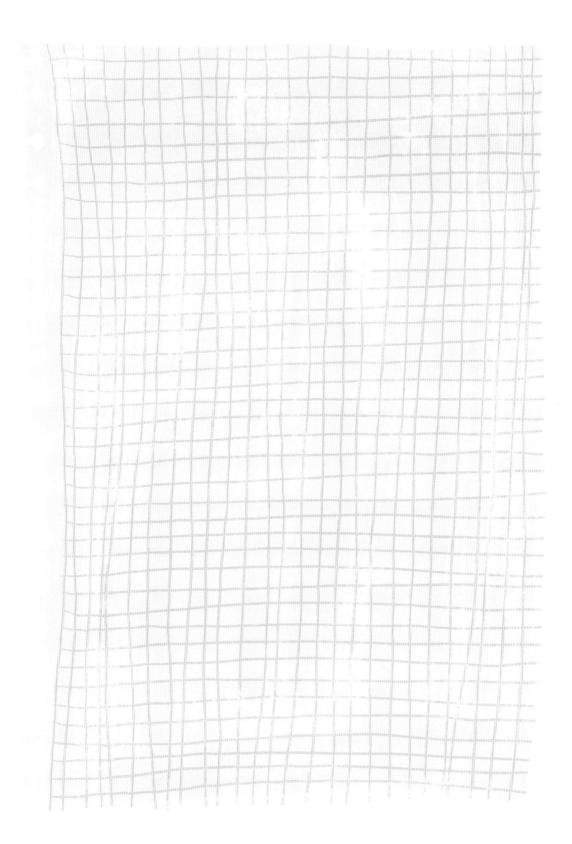

5
Gender Expression

Your gender expression is everything you do to express and communicate your gender identity. That includes a lot of different things. We'll look at them in a moment.

First, it's important for me to say: You are not only expressing your gender, other people also assume a gender when they see you.

This assumption by others does not have to match your gender identity. Even if other people assume you to be female/male – your gender is still determined by you alone!

Looking back through history, the "appropriate" way to express femininity or masculinity changed a lot!

Cultural context is also relevant. In some countries it is very common for men to wear clothing similar to a dress, or to wear jewelry, or hold hands as friends.

A man in a skirt-like piece of clothing isn't something "exotic." One widely known example from Europe would be Scotland. Though a lot of Scottish men would probably tell you that they are wearing a kilt, not a skirt. This is a good example of us assigning gender to clothes. (Why is the idea of a man wearing a skirt so unspeakable?)

Expressing your gender can mean different things.

Expression ranges from the more obvious stuff like clothes and hairstyles to piercings and tattoos.

Some people decide in favor of hormone treatment or plastic surgery to get closer to their preferred physical appearance. And that's not only trans people; cis people also use medical treatments if they want to make changes to their bodies!

Expressing your gender can be a very public action, like the examples just named. But it can also be something very private. Like painting your toe nails, just to figure out how it feels to have painted nails, but then hiding them with socks and shoes.

All of us are allowed to experiment with our expression - no matter what identity we have. And your gender expression doesn't have to be a stable thing that stays the same forever. You're allowed to change it whenever and just have fun with it.

Wear a dress.

Use makeup to paint on a beard.

You can do all this behind closed doors, just for yourself.

Or you get some friends together. You could even go out together.

Or you don't have to experiment at all. Maybe because you are afraid or because you already feel comfortable or for any other reason.
That's totally okay!

For some people gender expression can be connected to personal safety.

Some non-binary and genderqueer people might present in a more binary way when they navigate public spaces compared to their homes or when they're with friends. By doing so they avoid harassment in public restrooms, for example. The same goes for binary trans poeple who may feel pressured into putting in a greater effort to pass as cis in public spaces.

Trans people sometimes decide to present as their assigned gender because they fear violence if someone recognizes them as trans.

(These people are still trans! Again, your gender expression doesn't negate your gender identity.)

It would be so nice, though, if every person could just express themselves however they wanted to. Gender expression helps some people with their dysphoria.

Gender expression can also feel like breaking free from the gender binary and traditional gender roles.

For some people gender expression plays a huge role in feeling seen, connected, and supported.

You might not care about gender expression at all. Maybe you don't even see a connection between your gender and the way you express yourself. Or you just don't care. That's also fine.

LANGUAGE

Gender plays a huge role in our communication. Often we use gendered language, sometimes even without noticing it.

The way we talk influences our perception of the world around us. And our perception of the world influences how we act in it — so in a way our thoughts take part in shaping our reality.

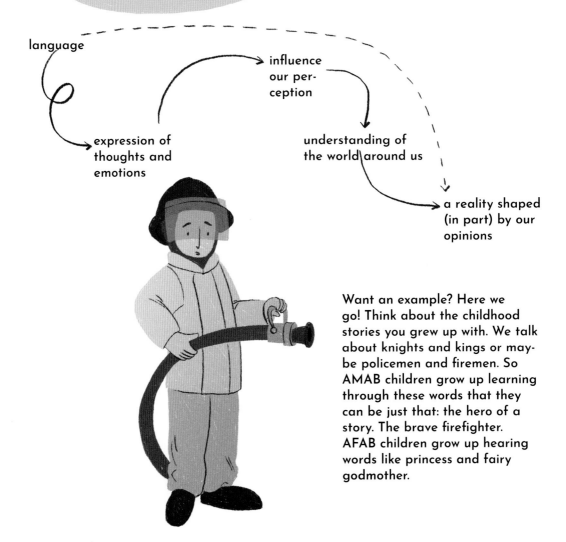

language

expression of thoughts and emotions

influence our perception

understanding of the world around us

a reality shaped (in part) by our opinions

Want an example? Here we go! Think about the childhood stories you grew up with. We talk about knights and kings or maybe policemen and firemen. So AMAB children grow up learning through these words that they can be just that: the hero of a story. The brave firefighter. AFAB children grow up hearing words like princess and fairy godmother.

But what about firewomen or fairy godfathers? These words immediately feel a little awkward, don't they? We don't expect girls in firemen costumes or boys wearing diadems. And non-binary people don't even appear in these words!

Our language reproduces the gender roles we looked at in chapter 3. This is easily rectified: We can adjust the way we talk, think, and shape reality! For example we can replace the word fireman with firefighter. Or fairy godmother with fairy godparent.

Of course nobody can force you to speak a certain way or use more inclusive language. But I do want to challenge you to a little experiment: Try to use gender-inclusive terms for a week and see what happens! When I did this I realized how much unconscious bias I still had. Word like "cleaning lady," "nurse," or "chairmen" were a huge struggle for me. And oh boy, does that say a lot about my ideas of gendered roles in society.

The names we use to address people or talk about them are also gendered in most cases. Most people get a name from their parents at birth.

Some people change their name at some point in their life. Maybe they start or stop using a nickname. Or they get a new family name after marriage.

Some people also use pseudonyms, for example on social media. But sex workers and authors also commonly work under different names.

Part of a social transition can be that a person picks a new name. Trans people who are close to their family sometimes include their parents in this process. Some ask friends. Others decide by themselves. The old and no longer used name is also called "deadname."

Getting used to a new name can take time. Maybe even the trans person them-self accidentally uses their deadname in the beginning. That is okay because everyone makes mistakes; it's only human.

But not even trying or refusing to use the new name is not only hurtful, it can be dangerous for the trans person if you out them publicly by doing this.

Whether you want to change your name, how you pick a new one, and who you tell about it: All of these are your decisions.

When we don't use a name to talk about a person we use pronouns. Pronouns are the little placeholders for someone's name we put in sentences. At school we learn "he" and "she" as options.

Some non-binary people don't feel comfortable with he/him or she/her pronouns. Being addressed with masculine or feminine language can be uncomfortable for people existing outside the binary.

They/them is a very established alternative in the English language. In 2015 the American Dialect Society even picked it as word of the year. About 300 linguists spoke up afterward and reaffirmed: Yes, they/them pronouns can be used in the singular form.

We do so all the time. For example when we tell a story and the gender isn't relevant. "They were so nice" is a sentence you can fully understand as referring to one person. Many non-binary and genderqueer people adopted they/them as their personal pronouns.
But there are more options than they/them.

THEY/
THEM

Here's an overview of pronouns a person might be using.
This list is incomplete and you should also take pronouns that don't appear on this list seriously. Some people may use pronouns in a different way than listed below. An example would be to combine pronouns and use she/they as identifiers. If you're not sure how to handle something: Ask the person how to talk about them. Pronouns are probably not the time to start a debate about grammar. A helpful rule of thumb: Go with the pronouns a person tells you regardless of your opinions.

he/him
This is my friend Charlie. I've known him for a long time; he was in school with me. Sometimes I watch his cat.

she/her
This is my friend Charlie. I've known her for a long time; she was in school with me. Sometimes I watch her cat.

they/them
This is my friend Charlie. I've known them for a long time; they were in school with me. Sometimes I watch their cat.

per/per
This is my friend Charlie. I've known per for a long time; per was in school with me. Sometimes I watch per cat.

xe/xem
This is my friend Charlie. I've known xem for a long time; xe was in school with me. Sometimes I watch xer cat.

ve/ver
This is my friend Charlie. I've known ver for a long time; ve was in school with me. Sometimes I watch ver cat.

First letter of the name
This is my friend Charlie. I've known C for a long time; C was in school with me. Sometimes I watch C's cat.

For trans people using the correct pronouns can be important to make them feel safe and supported.

When a person tells you which pronouns to use for them: put in a bit of an effort to actually use them. For the person asking it's probably not a small thing.

Okay.

As a cisgender person you can also help to normalize stating pronouns.

For example if a group meets for the first time you could ask everyone to not only state their name but also their pronouns.

Or just introduce yourself with your name and pronouns whenever you meet someone new.

If you're introducing yourself with your pronouns (of course only if you're comfortable doing so) there is less pressure on the people who don't use he/him or she/her pronouns. You immediately let them know that you are aware of the importance of pronouns and that you are willing to support them.

For some binary trans people it can be a really hard thing to be asked for pronouns.

They may not be able to answer the way they would want to, based on the context you're currently in. For example, they could be nervous because teachers or coworkers are close by who aren't supposed to know anything about their trans status (yet). Or maybe the question reminds them of a time when they couldn't pass and brings back emotions of dysphoria and trauma.

If you can do so you might be best off with opening up spaces to state pronouns without forcing anybody to do so. Cisgender people especially can use their privilege here and educate their fellow cis people.

Every person can use whichever pronouns they want to.

No pronoun "belongs" to any gender.

As a cisgender person you are welcome to use they/them pronouns.

Also all people are free to just "try on" pronouns. It doesn't have to be a lifelong and permanent choice. For example, you could ask your close friends to use a new pronoun for a while, just to get an idea of how it feels to you.

For other people it might be a bit confusing at first and they may struggle adjusting to many changes in pronouns.

That doesn't mean that you have less of a right to make these choices. And you do not have to feel guilty or ashamed when asking people to use the correct pronouns for you.

The only thing you really should avoid when it comes to pronouns: using them to make fun of trans people.

One example I actually heard in my past:

I now identify as car. You have to refer to me as car or I won't take anything you say about gender seriously.

This person probably wanted to express that they think pronouns like they/them are weird and useless. Which is an opinion you can have, fine, but that doesn't make it less important to others! And to put yourself over the needs of marginalized people isn't cool or funny – it's just being a douchebag.

BODIES

Most people have a complicated relationship with their own body, regardless of their gender.

The beauty norms in the Global North are simply unachievable. How we imagine the ideal body is a gendered thing.

The amount of curves a body is supposed to have, the height, the muscles — all of that is judged critically by others and ourselves.

And just to remind you of the diagram on page 49: Bodies and societies are not separately existing things. Our society influences our bodies. Our psyche influences our bodies. And the other way around is true as well.

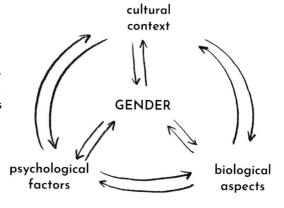

cultural
context

GENDER

psychological
factors

biological
aspects

For example, many people feel calmer when they exercise on a regular basis. Or they experience mood swings with their menstrual cycle.

Bodies are a complicated topic, every time and for everyone involved. It's okay if you sometimes feel uncomfortable in your body. Not every negative or complicated feeling has to do with gender.

That we express gender though our bodies has a lot to do with products being marketed to binary genders. It doesn't have to be this way and we should criticize this, as it is keeping the gender binary alive.

...Clothes, shoes, lingerie, accessories. The length of sleeves and shorts. Belts, hats, bags. Clothes are also heavily influenced by what is deemed to be "appropriate." So gender intersects once more with class, cultural or social context, religion, age, and race.

But as we currently live in this system, gender expression includes some of the following things:

...Scents. The deodorant or perfume you use is probably gendered. Some scents we associate more with masculinity, others with femininity.

...Lipstick, mascara, eyeliner, eyeshadow. All of these are products usually marketed only toward women.

...Body hair.

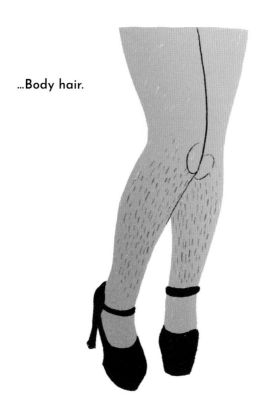

...Hairstyles

...Body language. Girls often get taught to sit still and make themselves small, while boys are encouraged to take up a lot of space.

Can you think of other things?

Our associating certain expressions with binary gender identities does not have to be the permanent status quo. Some non-binary folks struggle with figuring out a way to express themselves. Especially if they want to avoid being perceived as male or female. Many feminists hope for a world where dresses, skirts, and makeup are choices open to everyone, including men. We can all take small steps toward these goals. For one thing, if we're so inclined, by experimenting ourselves and becoming more playful in our expression. But also by accepting others and not judging them.

In case you don't feel comfortable experimenting in real life: Here's a dress-up doll. You can copy this page, color it in, cut it out, and play around. Enjoy!

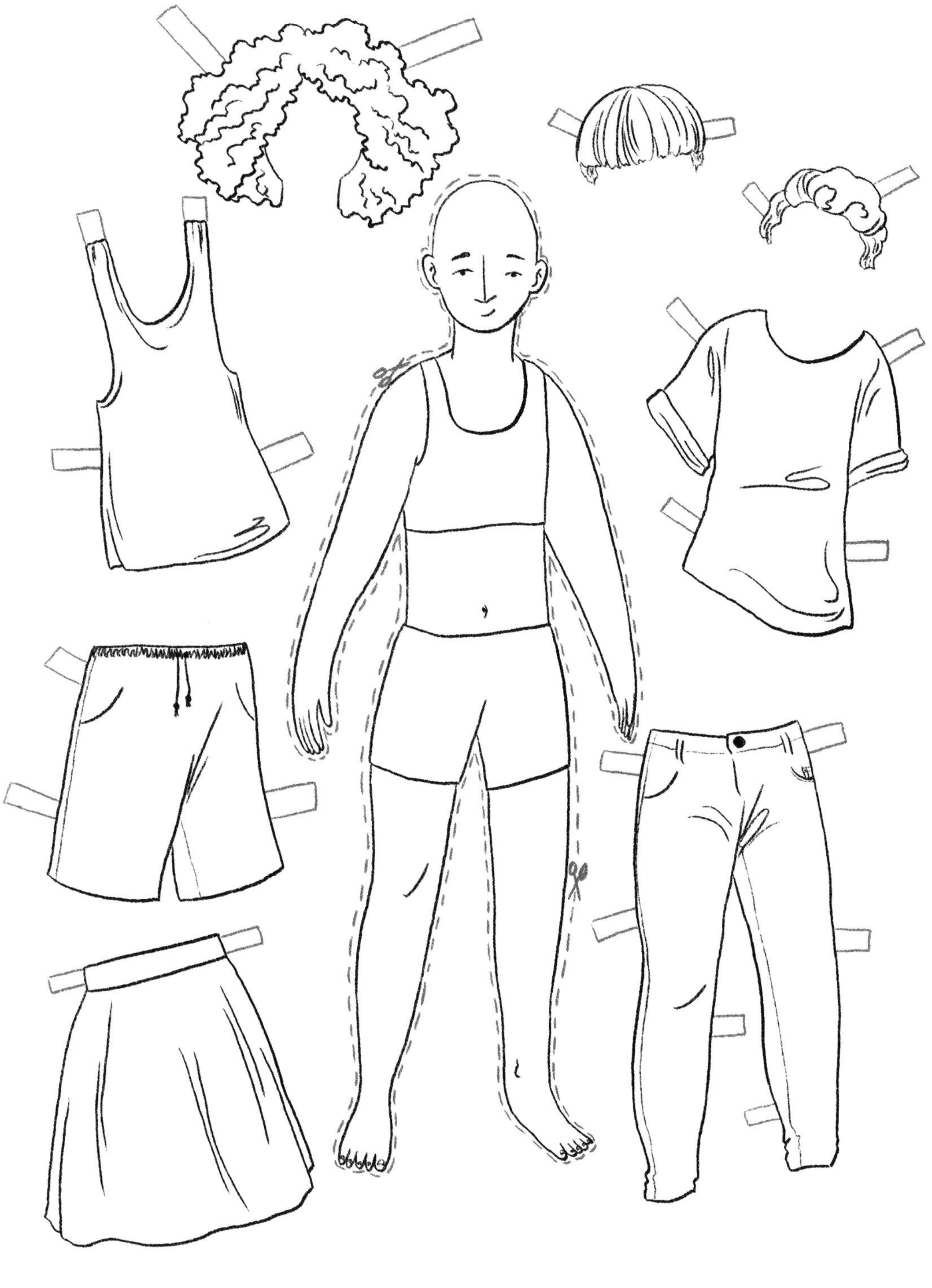

There is a term for this whole mess of us internalizing, perceiving, expressing, and reproducing the gender binary:

DOING GENDER

"Doing gender" means performing and expressing the social norms and expectations around gender. It describes the construction of gender as a process.

So we're no longer asking "What is a woman?" We're asking: "What makes a woman? Who makes her into one? What circumstances play a role? What is the goal here?"

Doing gender is happening all the time in our everyday lives. What are we wearing, how are we walking and standing, how do we present ourselves? Pretty much every activity you can think of comes with gendered expectations of how it should look.

Living in the gender binary also means: We are expected to perform gender. We can't just escape others assuming a gender when they see us. Just as we probably can't fully stop assuming the gender of others. (If you've managed to do that, I'm impressed!)

Doing gender is an interaction. We perform a gender, others perceive a gender, we perceive their gender as well, and so on. Reproducing the binary system easily becomes a very unconscious process with minimal effort we all participate in. Gender as a social construct gets made (or done or produced) in our everyday life.

Do you have ideas on how to rethink gender (expression)? How often and under which circumstances do you assume the gender identity of others? How can we break that cycle?

A type of performance art having a lot to do with gender and gender expression is drag.

DRAG

Drag queens and kings and quings intentionally perform an over-the-top version of gender expression.

The performance often is done in opposition to their own gender role. Nonetheless every person who wants to do drag can do so and there are women drag queens.

Some common stereotypes and misconceptions around drag are that only gay men do it or drag artists are secretly trans. Although drag is an art form that definitely bends the rules of gender and sexuality, not every drag artist is gay or trans. Yes, sometimes trans people figure out through doing drag that they are trans. But a lot of people just have fun with the art of drag. Or they want to inspire people to think about gender in new ways. Maybe they just want to entertain their audience, or make a political statement with their performance.

Space for your own notes:
Which expression makes you most comfortable? Can you think of situation when
you'd consider certain expressions inappropriate? Why? How are gender identity
and expression connected for you?

6
Coming Out / Inviting In

The term "coming out" describes the process of sharing your sexual orientation and/or gender identity with yourself and with others.

I am genderqueer.

Okay.

Pretty much only people from the LGBTQIA+ community have a coming out.

Straight people don't have to tell their friends, that they're straight. Cisgender people don't have to come out as cis.

The assumption that a person is straight and cis unless they come out is called cis-heteronormativity. The norm is to be cis and hetero. Everyone existing outside that norm has to explain themselves. (In case you can't tell by my face: I think that sucks.)

Instead of "coming out" some people prefer the term "inviting in." Using this term is an attempt at shifting the focus. Coming out means presenting yourself to a cis-heteronormative world. Inviting in is about trusting someone enough to be vulnerable, to share your authentic self.

Another term is "coming around." Coming out isn't a thing you do once and then you're done with it for the rest of your life. Talking about a coming around describes this experience as an ongoing process. A person who is coming around is doing so over and over again — whenever they meet someone new, start a new job, move to a new place, there will be a coming around. Coming around isn't a widely known concept, though. I picked it up in some German-speaking communities. In other countries it may not be commonly known as a term.

When we are talking about coming out, what are we actually saying? What are we coming out of? What are we going into?

The idea of a coming out is often criticized. Because we only need to come out as long as we believe that being cis, being straight is normal and doesn't need to be communicated.

People who are not cis and/or straight are constantly confronted with the expectation to explain and share their personal experiences. Oftentimes they have to deal with negativity, hate, and discrimination when doing so. Need examples? Trans people often get asked about their genitalia and surgery plans. Lesbian people get questions and comments on their sex life. Even by complete strangers. We would not accept these questions after a person says "oh, by the way, I'm straight."

Those are only two examples of bad responses to someone coming out. The lives of queer people are full of them. That's why I've put together a list of ideas on how to handle a coming around/inviting in. This list is incomplete and not in any order. Also: You don't have to do all of these things (at once)!

- Be patient. Give the person the space to share in their own time. Sometimes someone just wants to get it off their chest. Other times someone doesn't really want to talk about it. Don't force anyone into a conversation they are not ready for.

- Take the trust this person put in you seriously. Respect their privacy. Telling others about this is not cool; please don't gossip. Also try to recognize the risk the person took with you. Don't downplay the importance or difficulty of a coming out. "This doesn't change anything for me, I don't care about gender" might not be the best thing to hear for some people.

- Thank them for their trust.

- Instead of saying "It doesn't matter./It's not important," try: "This doesn't change how I feel about you." Or maybe even say that you feel your connection is closer because of their vulnerability around you.

- Try not to judge. If you fundamentally question the existence of someone's identity or you find it hard to accept it because of values or religious beliefs: This is probably not the best time to say so. You will have a lot of time later on to have loving and caring conversations about your questions, doubts, and conflicts.

- Ask the person if they want a hug.

- Ask the person if the need/want your support with anything.

- Ask for pronouns and names. Also check in with them about social bubbles where the person isn't out yet. Make sure you won't bring up their queerness in these settings.

- Educate yourself. Don't expect the person who just invited you in to now also be your personal tutor. Research their identity, maybe watch a video on YouTube. Small gestures go a long way. Show the person that you are curious about their experience – but also aware that they don't have to do the work for you.

- Include the person in your plans. It is possible that the person lost friends or family by coming around/inviting in. They might need you to just be present.

- Do whatever it is you did before. If you had a phone call every day or went for a weekly coffee – continue doing just that. Show the person that your relationship is still intact.

When talking about coming around/inviting in you may hear the term "inner" and "outer" coming out.

The inner coming out is the coming out to oneself.

It means you become aware of your own gender.

HELLO, I AM...
QUEER

Coming out to oneself can be a very long and difficult process. This process is even harder for people who do not have access to the information they'd need to understand what's going on. Or people who live in a household with a transphobic person. Or people who don't have access to safer spaces to talk about their emotions and struggles.

Coming out to yourself in no way means you have to share this knowledge with someone. Or change something. Or do anything really. If you want to do so: Remind yourself that you are allowed to do everything at your own pace. You can take one step at a time or all of them at once. But you are under no obligation to share your private thoughts with everyone.

After coming out to myself I didn't come out to anyone else for about five years. First I didn't want to accept I was trans. Then I just bottled it up. I didn't experience dysphoria to a point where I couldn't handle everyday life anymore. So even when I finally shared with friends, I still was coming out to myself. Luckily everyone reacted wonderfully and supported me. I needed to feel the euphoria of my friends using my new name and pronouns and taking me shopping to finally begin accepting myself.

Coming out to myself was never an issue for me. My experience fits the narrative of the trans person who knew as a child that something was off. Sharing it like this doesn't sit well with me. I don't want to reaffirm this cliché. I want to see and read more stories of trans people who struggled, who took a while, who are unsure or only later in life find out they are trans. And at the same time I do think it's important to share coming around stories like mine - the incredibly boring ones. To encourage people. And show them: It doesn't have to be dramatic. Sometimes coming around as trans is just very chill.

I've known for a while now that I am non-binary. I have not yet shared this with friends or family. When I talked to them about gender identities on a more abstract level it became clear that all of them have a negative attitude toward the topic. Or don't even believe it's a real thing. Now I am scared they will react badly when I come out.

I felt way too much pressure to have all the answers and be completely certain before coming out. Coming out already requires a lot of courage - so naturally I wanted to seem confident and authentic. By now I kind of wish I hadn't pressured myself that much. Finding clarity about your identity, that's a lifelong process.

The outer com-
ing out/coming
around/inviting in
is the process of
sharing your iden-
tity with others.

You probably will never
be done with your outer
coming out. You constant-
ly meet new people. And
some of them might become
friends and maybe at some
point you'll want to talk
about these things. But
nobody should force you to
come out to them.

For a lot of people the thought of sharing their identity is scary at first. Especially right at the beginning
when you might be insecure yourself and everything
still feels new. It's okay to be worried about negative
reactions.

Inviting in your own family feels like the biggest risk to
some people. These are the people who've known us the
longest and whose rejection could hurt us the most.

If your family responds
with hatred, violence, or in any other
negative way: know that it is not your
fault and there is nothing wrong with
you. In the very back of the book is a
list of places where you can find help.

My mom doesn't believe I'm a boy to this day. She still uses my deadname and buys dresses for me and things like that. Before I came out as trans we were close. Since then our relationship is more distant. Both of us pretend I never came out and we avoid all personal topics. Sometimes I wish I never came out to her. But I had to choose one: Share my true self or have a good relationship with my mother.

My family is very religious. A lot of them didn't talk with me for months after my coming out. There also was tension between my parents, my siblings, and me. The other day my aunt said god made me this way for a reason. It was one of the most beautiful things she could have said, even though I don't believe in God myself.

My parents reacted really well. I was so nervous when I told them! My mom told me she doesn't fully understand but supports everything that makes me happy. My dad just gave me a long hug.

My parents kicked me out after I invited them in. Well, not immediately after. There were talks about therapy first and a lot of arguments. But in the end it was clear: We cannot live together anymore. I'm still not fully over it. Your family is supposed to be a place of unconditional love and yet mine can't accept me the way I am. I moved in with my grandma after. She always said she doesn't want to know, she just wants me to be happy. Her support couldn't heal what my parents did. I'm not in contact with them anymore.

In school or at work the legal transition (p. 90) is more important than it should be.

Many institutions refuse to use a different name than the one on legal documents. For trans people who haven't yet gone through the legal transition finding a job can be really hard because of that. Another difficulty could be school: gym classes are sometimes separated by gender. So are school uniforms.

In these contexts coming out can be really important for someone. Simultaneously it can be terrifying because your education, degree, or financial situation might be affected by it.

I was so lucky with my uni. When I came out the head of faculty wrote an e-mail to all lecturers explaining my name should be changed on all class documents. My student ID still has my old name on it because I haven't changed my ID yet. But the mail address from my university is correct and everyone in my classes tries hard to use my name and I feel so privileged because people keep checking in: What do you need, how can we support you?

I used to keep my being inter a secret. Only since there has been some public debate, and now with the third legal gender option in Germany, I think about it more and more. I am considering changing my name and talked with my friends about it. In some ways my position might be easier because I can say: "This is my body, this is real and it always has been like this." On the other hand a lot of people still don't know what intersex means. So whenever I want to come out I also have to educate others.

Everyone besides my boss knows I'm non-binary. It isn't a huge deal for any of them. Sure, in the beginning there were a lot of questions. And some still don't understand what it means to me. But overall I didn't have negative experiences until now. I'd love to come out at work. My boss though, he made homo- and transphobic "jokes" several times and I am scared of losing my job.

I wasn't out in school at first. One day our gym teacher announced it's girls against boys. So the girls went to the one side, boys to the other and I stood awkwardly in the middle. When the teacher asked what's up, I whispered that I didn't know my gender. I was referee after that and the whole thing was done.

My friends in school responded well enough when I came out as agender. They were confused at first but they weren't mean or anything like that. A couple days later they discussed it in a lunch break, I think they just had a lot of questions. But by doing so they shared my identity with the whole class. For a whole year everyone laughed about me, many students didn't believe agender people exist and mocked me. There were moments when students blocked my access to the restroom because I'm not a girl. People just called me a hermaphrodite. It took a while but eventually everyone calmed down. The friendships I used to have didn't survive all this.

Nobody has a right to listen to your story. It is your story. Whom you trust enough to invite them in is completely your decision.

Space for your own notes:
Do you talk about your gender identity? With whom? How do they respond? Are there people in your life that make you question gender roles or your gender identity? Why? How do you feel when you think about a coming out/inviting in? How do you expect people in your life to react if you ever bring up gender as a topic? How would you yourself like to react?

7
Now What?

So... this was a lot. And possibly a lot of new information for you. What you do with all this knowledge now, that's up to you.

Maybe you've had enough of this topic by now. Totally fine with me. There are a lot of interesting topics out there you can dive into next. For some people gender is super important – and for others, not so much.

Maybe you want to learn more. I've got some tips for further reading on the last pages. Maybe you just have to take a breath and process.

But in case you're asking yourself right now: "What do I do with all this information!? What does it mean for my personal life?" I've got some ideas!

Accept yourself the way you are. Try to detach yourself from the ideals, norms, and ideas you have about your gender role.

Question yourself on a regular basis: Are your decisions based on your own needs or determined by gendered expectations?

Don't rush yourself. Understanding gender takes time, if it's even possible at all. It's not going to happen over night.

Try not to assume the gender of people you've just met. And yes, that includes people who present in line with traditional gender roles.

Introduce yourself to new people with your name and your pronouns.

Recognize your privilege. Maybe even start trying to uplift the voices of people with less privilege. Listen to their stories and share them with others.

Stand up against sexism, homophobia, and transphobia. (If you feel safe in that situation!)

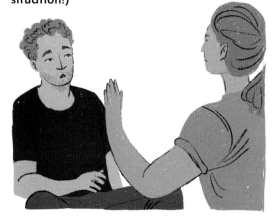

Try to identify your own internalized and unconscious bias. All of us grew up with sexism and the norm to be straight and cis. So it's 100% normal to have all of that somewhere in our brains. All of us still have to (un-)learn.

Ask yourself every now and then why we (as a society) do things a certain way. Could we do it differently? Where did this norm come from? Whom does it serve?

Rethink gendered actions. Why should it be boys asking for the first date? Why is it girls who need to help with household chores?

Reaffirm that objects don't have a gender. Clothes, hairstyles, nail polish, deodorant, toys, and similar gendered items can be used by anyone.

If you find yourself outside of cisgender heterosexual norms and want to do so: Go and find your community. There are a lot of people who share your identity, online and offline, whom you can talk to.

Do you have other ideas?

Start talking with friends about gender. All of us have a gender role and identity, and talking about it, sharing experiences and thoughts, that's probably a really helpful and cool thing to do.

How are you after reading all this? Write down your feelings and thoughts running through your head. What did you learn? Are there aspects of gender you want to learn more about? What's your takeaway from this book? This is your space for all the notes you couldn't fit in anywhere else.

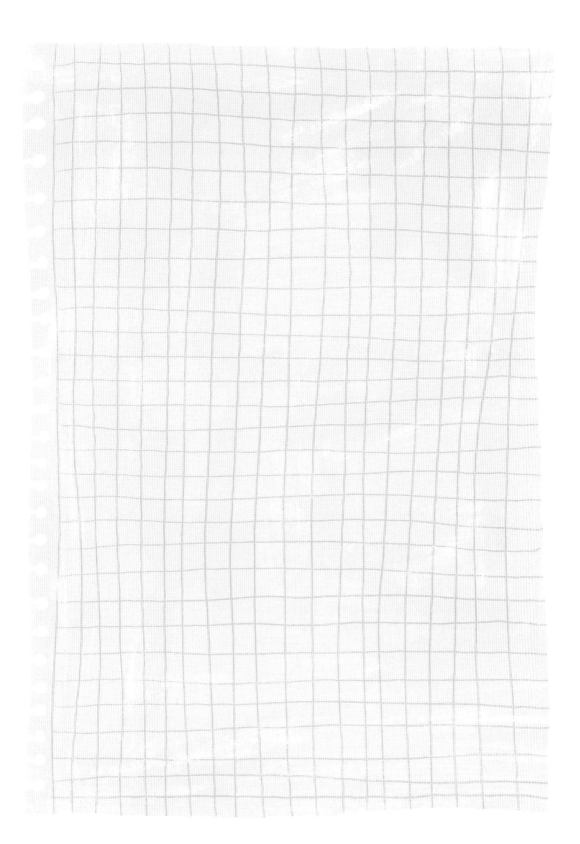

RESOURCES

The Trevor Project
A suicide prevention and crisis intervention organization for LGBTQIA+ youth
https://www.thetrevorproject.org/

Trans Lifeline
A trans peer support for and by trans people
US (877) 565-8860
Canada (877) 330-6366

LGBT foundation
To support LGBTQIA+ people in the UK
https://lgbt.foundation/
Helpline: 0345 3 30 30 30

Life Outside the Binary
A non-binary and trans information center
https://lifeoutsidethebinary.com/

National Domestic Violence Hotline (US)
https://www.thehotline.org/
1 800 799 7233 or text "START" to 88788

National Domestic Abuse Helpline (UK)
https://www.nationaldahelpline.org.uk/
0808 2000 247

The Men's Advice Line, for male domestic abuse survivors (UK)
0808 801 0327

YOUTUBE

Kat Blaque   Jamie Dodger   Contra Points   Upper Case Chase

Ash Hardell   Jackson Bird   Riley J. Dennis

BOOKS

- *To My Trans Sister*, Charlie Cragg
- *Man Alive*, Thomas Page McBee
- *Trans Bodies, Trans Selves*, Laura Erickson-Schroth
- *Paul Takes the Form of A Mortal Girl*, Andrea Lawlor
- *I'm Afraid of Men*, Vivek Shraya
- *Uncomfortable Labels: My Life as a Gay Autistic Trans Woman*, Laura Kate Dale
- *Black on Both Sides: A Racial History of Trans Identity*, C. Riley Snorton
- *Detransition, Baby*, Torrey Peters
- *Beyond the Gender Binary*, Alok Vaid-Menon
- *How to Understand your Gender: A practical guide for exploring who you are*, Alex Iantaffi and Meg-John Barker
- *Trans Power: Owen Your Gender*, edited by Juno Roche
- *Life Isn't Binary: On Being Both, Beyond, and In-Between*, Alex Iantaffi and Meg-John Barker
- *Non-Binary Lives: An Anthology of Intersecting Identities*, edited by Jos Twist, Ben Vincent, Meg-John Barker and Kat Gupta
- *Gender Explorerers: Our Stories of Growing Up Trans and Changing the World*, edited by Juno Roche
- *Spectrums: Autistic Transgender People in Their Own Words*, edited by Maxfield Sparrow
- *Gender Queer*, Maia Kobabe

You have now reached the end of this book. (Congrats, pat yourself on the back!) I hope you read this page with some new thoughts and ideas - but mostly with a lot of curiosity and questions. Thank you for taking the time to read all this. Thank you for paying attention.

A huge "thank you" goes out to all the people who allowed me to share their stories here. Within one year I posed the same questions about gender to roughly 100 people. To each of them: Thank you for your vulnerability, your willingness to share, and your support.

And thank you to Lou, whom I dedicated this book to. You helped me sort through my own struggles with gender and your friendship means the world to me.